Praise for *Blogging to Drive Business*

W9-ARV-472

"A great read! If you're looking to start a blog for your business, this is the book for you. It's well-written and comprehensive, including case studies and examples of real companies to make the concepts easy to understand."

—**Dee Barizo**, performancing.com

"*Blogging to Drive Business* does an excellent job at educating the market on the critical elements required for success in the digital economy. After all, businesses only gain market share when they communicate in a way that enhances relationships. *Blogging to Drive Business* provides the roadmap for success!"

—**Jay Deragon**, Social Media Strategist

"This book provides business owners and entrepreneurs hands-on advice on starting a blog—why planning is important, who should be contributing, what tools are available, and where to find additional resources and content ideas. The authors make good use of case studies to address many of the commonly asked questions about blogging. If you've been on the fence about starting a blog, this book will help you draw an action plan."

—**Valeria Maltoni**, Conversation Agent

"Butow and Bollwitt have assembled a practical guide for any company to follow as they develop a blogging strategy. Their approach is firmly planted in driving business success without overburdening executives with impractical advice or ideological mantras. I highly recommend this book for anyone who wants to take advantage of a blogging strategy to promote their business and connect with prospective and current customers."

—**Jeff Nolan**, Venture Chronicles

"If you are looking for a practical guide to show you exactly how to use a blog to drive business, look no further, you've found it. As a practioner myself, I know there are some skills that can only be learned by doing. These authors know what they're talking about because they've done it. Save yourself some time and invest in this book."

—**Michelle Price**, CEO, A Third Mind Digital Media

"If you get blogging right, it can be a major benefit for you business. This book helps you get the strategy and planning right upfront, and then talks you through the steps you need to make your blog a success and to grow and develop it."

—**Matt Rhodes**, FreshNetworks

"*Blogging to Drive Business* is a no-nonsense and practical guide for those who have yet to embark on the road to enhanced corporate communications. It explains why, who, what, and how to start and maintain a valuable connection with your customers via this engaging medium."

—**Hayden Sutherland**, Ideal Interface (UK)

BLOGGING

Create and Maintain Valuable Customer Connections

TO DRIVE BUSINESS

Eric Butow & Rebecca Bollwitt

800 East 96th Street,
Indianapolis, Indiana 46240 USA

Blogging to Drive Business
Create and Maintain Valuable Customer Connections

Copyright © 2010 by Pearson Education, Inc.

All rights reserved. No part of this book shall be reproduced, stored
in a retrieval system, or transmitted by any means, electronic, mechan-
ical, photocopying, recording, or otherwise, without written permission from the publisher. No patent liability is assumed with respect to
the use of the information contained herein. Although every precau-
tion has been taken in the preparation of this book, the publisher and
author assume no responsibility for errors or omissions. Nor is any
liability assumed for damages resulting from the use of the information contained herein.

ISBN-13: 978-0-7897-4256-8
ISBN-10: 0-7897-4256-X

Library of Congress Cataloging-in-Publication data is on file

Printed in the United States of America

First Printing: January 2010

Trademarks

All terms mentioned in this book that are known to be trademarks or
service marks have been appropriately capitalized. Que Publishing
cannot attest to the accuracy of this information. Use of a term in this
book should not be regarded as affecting the validity of any trademark
or service mark.

Warning and Disclaimer

Every effort has been made to make this book as complete and as
accurate as possible, but no warranty or fitness is implied. The information provided is on an "as is" basis. The authors and the publisher
shall have neither liability nor responsibility to any person or entity
with respect to any loss or damages arising from the information contained in this book.

Bulk Sales

Que Publishing offers excellent discounts on this book when ordered
in quantity for bulk purchases or special sales. For more information,
please contact

U.S. Corporate and Government Sales
1-800-382-3419
corpsales@pearsontechgroup.com

For sales outside of the U.S., please contact

International Sales
international@pearson.com

Associate Publisher
Greg Wiegand

Acquisitions Editor
Michelle Newcomb

Development Editor
Ginny Bess Munroe

Managing Editor
Kristy Hart

Project Editor
Andy Beaster

Copy Editor
Keith Cline

Indexer
Lisa Stump

Proofreader
Seth Kerney

Technical Editor
Paul Chaney

Publishing Coordinator
Cindy Teeters

Interior Designer
Anne Jones

Cover Designer
Anne Jones

Compositor
Gloria Schurick

CONTENTS AT A GLANCE

TABLE OF CONTENTS

About the Authors

Eric Butow is CEO of Butow Communications Group (BCG), a Web design and online marketing firm in Jackson, California. Eric has written a wide variety of computing books since 2000, and his latest titles include *User Interface Design for Mere Mortals, How to Succeed in Business Using LinkedIn,* as well as custom For Dummies titles for F5 Networks and Hewlett-Packard. When Eric isn't writing or running his business, you'll catch him reading and enjoying the weather of the Sierra foothills.

Rebecca Bollwitt is the co-founder of sixty4media, which specializes in WordPress design and development as well as social media consulting in Vancouver, British Columbia. Rebecca has been blogging since 2004 on Miss604.com, and podcasting about music and hockey since 2005. Miss604.com was voted "Best Vancouver Blog" of 2009 in *The Georgia Straight* and in 2008, she was listed within the top ten "Most Influential in Canadian Social Media" by Profectio.com. She has organized social media conferences and charity fundraisers, including Blogathon Vancouver, Twestival Local, and the Best of 604 Awards.

Dedication

From Eric: To Katie Sullivan: You have the whole universe ahead of you, and you'll have fun exploring with your wonderful parents, Laura and James.

From Rebecca: To John, you are my best friend and my motivation. For my mother, sister, and Oma; three of the strongest women I'll ever know.

Acknowledgments

From Eric: Thanks to my coauthor, Rebecca Bollwitt, for being such a pleasure to work with. Ginny Munroe and Michelle Newcomb at Que made the editing and authoring process really easy. And I want to give a big shout out to the best literary agent in the world—Carole Jelen of Waterside Productions. To all of you and to everyone at Que responsible for making this book a reality, thank you.

From Rebecca: Thank you to Eric Butow for being an inspirational coauthor, Ginny Munroe and Michelle Newcomb for their kindness, and everyone at Que for making this book a reality. Thank you Carole Jelen of Waterside for taking a chance on this Canadian girl and one big hat tip to the Vancouver social media community.

We Want to Hear from You!

As the reader of this book, *you* are our most important critic and commentator. We value your opinion and want to know what we're doing right, what we could do better, what areas you'd like to see us publish in, and any other words of wisdom you're willing to pass our way.

As an associate publisher for Que Publishing, I welcome your comments. You can email or write me directly to let me know what you did or didn't like about this book—as well as what we can do to make our books better.

Please note that I cannot help you with technical problems related to the topic of this book. We do have a User Services group, however, where I will forward specific technical questions related to the book.

When you write, please be sure to include this book's title and author, as well as your name, email address, and phone number. I will carefully review your comments and share them with the author and editors who worked on the book.

Email: feedback@quepublishing.com

Mail: Greg Wiegand
         Associate Publisher
         Que Publishing
         800 East 96th Street
         Indianapolis, IN 46240 USA

Reader Services

Visit our website and register this book at informit.com/register for convenient access to any updates, downloads, or errata that might be available for this book.

Introduction

Blogs represent a great opportunity for businesses to get their names out into cyberspace as experts in their line of work. Often, however, businesses don't know where to start or about potential pitfalls (for example, how to attract the most people to their blog, what to say, and perhaps more important, what not to say).

Blogging to Drive Business *will help businesses of any size learn more about blogging, from both the technical and strategic perspectives. After all, you need the specific technical instructions to set up your blog and add information to it, and you need to know how to get eyeballs looking at your blogs and how to leverage your blog with your other online (and offline) marketing efforts.*

How This Book Is Organized

There's a lot of material to cover, but we cover it step by step through nine chapters:

- **Chapter 1, "Why Are Blogs So Important?"** covers blog basics, how blogs can help you serve customers better, and how to use blogs to get more information about your customers.

- **Chapter 2, "Leveraging Your Blog with Marketing Tools,"** shows you how to build an integrated online and offline marketing toolbox that includes blogs. You'll also learn how to push your blog information to your customers, pull customers to your blog, and take care of your readers.

- **Chapter 3, "Creating a Blogging Strategy,"** gets into the nuts and bolts of blogging. You learn about popular blogging platforms, how to find the blogs that are best for your business, and how to combine blogs with other networking sites such as Facebook, LinkedIn, and Twitter.

- **Chapter 4, "Blogging Responsibly,"** explains how you need to listen to your audience to be an effective blogger and how to respond professionally to comments made to your blog posts.

- **Chapter 5, "Finding Topics to Write About,"** answers the question about how to write topics on a regular basis to keep your audience engaged and coming back for more. You also learn about how to create one or more internal blogs for your company.

- **Chapter 6, "Who Will Write the Blog?"** identifies ways to find one or more people within your company to write a blog. Your writer can be someone who is already on your staff, such as the marketing manager (perhaps with a message from the CEO on a regular basis), or you can hire a professional blogger. This chapter also explains how to write effective blog posts.

- **Chapter 7, "Getting Eyeballs to Your Blog,"** tells you how to get your blog noticed. Start by reading blogs so that you can see how other companies in your industry blog successfully. The chapter then examines how to link your blog and make it searchable, how to get crowd-powered content, and how to promote your blog using other marketing techniques such as press releases and your company Web site.

- **Chapter 8, "Getting Interactive with Multimedia Blogging,"** shows how to create podcasts and screencasts, post them on a blog, and how to create multimedia blogs for different audiences.

- **Chapter 9, "Taking Advantage of Web 3.0 Blogs,"** provides an overview of Web 3.0 technologies so that you can be ahead of the curve as we enter the second decade of the twenty-first century. This chapter also explains how to integrate Web 3.0 technologies such as the Semantic Web into your blog.

- **Appendix A, "Important Blogging Sites,"** is a good place to start if you want to see where people go when they want blogging platforms or want their blogs to get noticed. Many of the sites in this appendix are also discussed in this book.

In every chapter of this book, we've included at least one example of how companies use blogs effectively (or, in some cases, ineffectively). Our examples give you a good idea of what you can do (and what you shouldn't do) for your business blogs. At the very least, these examples will get your creative juices flowing.

Conventions Used in This Book

We hope that this book is easy enough to follow intuitively. As you read through the pages, however, it helps to know precisely how we've presented specific types of information.

Web Pages

Obviously, this book contains a lot of Web page addresses, like this one: www.wordpress.com. When you see one of these addresses (also known as a URL), you can go to that Web page by entering the URL into the address box in your Web browser. We have made every effort to ensure the accuracy of the Web addresses presented here. Given the ever-changing nature of the Web, however, don't be surprised if you run across an address or two that have changed since this book was published.

Special Elements

As you read through this book you'll note several special elements, presented in what people in the publishing business call *margin notes*. There are different types of margin notes for different types of information, as you see here.

 Note

This is a note that presents some interesting information, even if it isn't wholly relevant to the discussion in the main text.

🔍 Tip

This is a tip that might prove useful for whatever it is you're in the process of doing.

There's More Online

To provide you the most up-to-date information about blogging to supplement (and sometimes correct) what you find in this book, we've set up a Web site at www.blog2drivebiz.com. This site is... a blog! It's also a great place to get more information from Eric and Rebecca about what's going on in the blogosphere.

You can also visit Eric's business Web site (www.butow.net) and Rebecca's business Web site (www.sixty4media.com) to learn more about books we've written, upcoming speaking engagements, and yes, to read our blogs.

Now that you know how to use this book, it's time to learn why blogs are so important to your business marketing strategy, a subject we cover in the opening chapter.

1

Why Are Blogs So Important?

You might have picked up this book because you have seen a blog on a Web site you frequent. Or maybe you've heard about the term blog *used by the media; after all, it's a huge buzzword, and some people believe that it is important for a business to have one. In any case, you might not know what a blog is exactly and why it's so important for your business to have one. So, this chapter explains what a blog is and how you can use blogs to promote your business and gather more information about your customers.*

Media Growth Is in One Area: Online

With all the attention paid to the Web during the past decade and a half, you know that the Web has become, for many people, a preferred way to get information. This preference comes at the expense of more traditional media such as radio, television, and newspapers. For instance, at the time of this writing, the newspaper industry is contracting, and those in the newspaper/media business are openly wondering whether printed newspapers will even exist in 2020.

Improvements in computing technology and connection speeds have made traditional media content accessible on the Web as never before, and at prices that are reasonable or even free. Therefore, Eric dropped his package of TV, Internet, and phone access because he already had a cell phone, a mobile GSM card, and Wi-Fi for Web access, and he can get his favorite shows on video sites such as YouTube and Hulu.

In addition, many people are bypassing traditional media entirely and are reading content on the Web, and some are even creating content of their own. One popular way users create content is via a blog, which is short for *Web log*. You can integrate other technologies into a blog; for example, social networking functionality, your Web site, a hosted blogging Web site, such as WordPress, or a combination of these. (The next section considers these combos in more detail.)

And here's the kicker: Online media is the only area of media currently growing. As that growth accelerates, people are finding more and more different kinds of information online. Blogs are increasingly popular, too. In fact, Technorati (http://www.technorati.com), which tracks blogs, noted in its 2008 "State of the Blogosphere" report that more than 77 million unique visitors read blogs in the United States alone (see Figure 1.1).

Even so, these factoids don't tell you why people, especially businesspeople, create blogs. So let's start at the beginning: What is a blog good for, anyway?

Get the Message Out

A blog is an online journal that you can keep on your own Web site, house on a site specifically designed to host blogs (see Appendix A, "Important Blogging Sites," for a list of the important ones), or produce on a social networking Web site such as MySpace that offers blog functionality. Like many computing technologies before it, blogging enables people to communicate with large numbers of people quickly and publicly. Bloggers may also produce and publish content anonymously (in case they want to write about hot-button issues, such as politics, without people learning their true identities). For example, one of Eric's favorite blogs is the Halfway There blog shown in Figure 1.2; a friend of Eric's, who uses the pseudonym Zeno Ferox, writes it.

Figure 1.1 *The Technorati 2008 "State of the Blogosphere" report.*

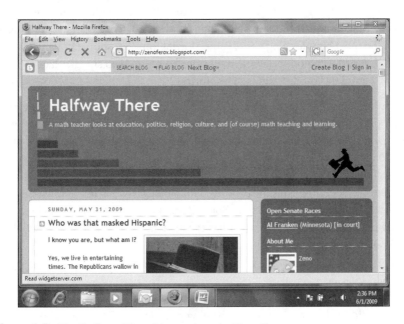

Figure 1.2 *The Halfway There blog, written by Zeno Ferox.*

Blog Popularity

People have been blogging since Web browsers became widely available in the mid-1990s, and blogs have steadily become more popular since then. A September 24, 2008 article on the Ars Technica Web site (http://arstechnica.com/old/content/2008/09/blog-growth-slows-more-bloggers-are-bringing-home-the-bacon.ars) illustrates just how quickly the number of blogs Technorati tracked between 2005 and 2008 grew. In 2005, the number was 8 million. In 2006, the number grew more than fourfold to 35 million. In 2007, the number of blogs more than doubled to 72 million. In 2008, Technorati reported it was tracking 133 million blogs.

The Technorati 2008 "State of the Blogosphere" report identified how many users have blogs on the two largest social networking Web sites; as of 2008, Facebook had 41 million bloggers, and MySpace had 75 million. This difference in numbers might be because MySpace built blogging capabilities into its system early on in its development, whereas Facebook blogs were an add-on (and not too easy to find on the site as of this writing).

So, which blogs are the most popular? It depends on what source you use to measure blog popularity. Technorati lists its up-to-date top 100 blogs on its Web site by authority (that is, the number of comments posted on the blog, which notes the level of user activity) or by the number of fans who have bothered to vote for their favorite blog on the Technorati site. When we checked Technorati in early August 2009, the most popular blog site was the Huffington Post, shown in Figure 1.3 (http://www.huffingtonpost.com), a news and opinion Web site that had more than 18,000 comments on its various news stories.

According to a 2009 Google case study (http://www.google.com/analytics/case_study_huffington_post.html), the Huffington Post has surpassed 8 million unique visitors just in 2009 as of August 2009, which is considerable considering that the top 25 most popular blogs account for more than 10 percent of blog readership according to the ComScore Web traffic measurement firm (http://www.smartmoney.com/spending/rip-offs/10-things-your-blogger-wont-tell-you-20825/). However, Technorati considers the Boing Boing blog (http://www.boingboing.net) as the most popular blog because it has the most fans—that is, the number of Technorati readers who read it.

Hello, World!

So, how did businesses learn about the blog phenomenon? In many cases, employees talked about their own blogs. Employees kept track of what was going on with marketing and customers learned about blogging. And the mainstream media picked up on blogging, especially as people started turning to blogs such as Ars Technica (http://www.arstechnica.com) for technical news, as shown in Figure 1.4.

All this information was passed along to C-level executives in the business, which in turn got businesses thinking about how they could make their businesses known in the blogosphere.

Figure 1.3 The Huffington Post site.

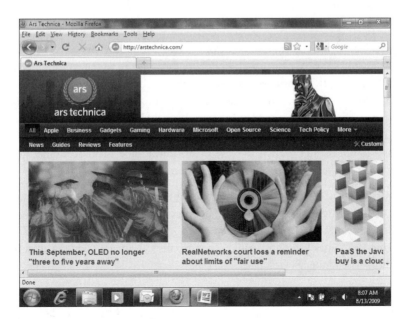

Figure 1.4 The Ars Technica Web site.

The Technorati 2008 report noted that dilettantes, who might write only once in a while (or on a whim), were writing fewer and fewer blogs. Instead, professional or corporate bloggers are taking over much of the blogosphere. These professionals write for money on blogging sites such as Ars Technica and may also perform other duties for a company (for example, an engineer or a marketing person, such as for the Intel Inside Scoop blog that we talk about in this chapter's case study).

The professionalization of blogging has attracted advertisers who pay a price to have their banner ad on the blog. For example, Eric's company blog might have a banner ad from the photographer he works with to help drive business to her company, and the photographer can also have a link on her Web site to Eric's blog so that it benefits both companies. The 2008 Technorati blogging report noted that most bloggers accept advertising on their blogs, with a mean annual revenue of $6,000. Blogging sites that have more than 100,000 unique visitors a month can command much higher rates, with a mean annual revenue of $75,000.

You learn more about writing your blogs in Chapter 5, "Finding Topics to Write About," and Chapter 6, "Who Will Write the Blog?"

Promote Products and Services

Blogging can be an additional income source, and perhaps even lucrative if you dedicate the resources necessary to build it up. But after you create your blog, what then? The most immediate use of a blog is to talk about your products and services. The conversation benefits not just your existing customers but also potential customers who might have questions about your company and its products/services.

If you offer general information and commentary about the state of your industry or profession, your blog can also highlight your expertise to the community at large. For example, suppose you use Rubbermaid products and want to get additional information about how to use them to organize your life more effectively. You can just go to the Adventures in Organization blog, shown in Figure 1.5. This blog discusses general organizational issues and problems and tips about how you can use Rubbermaid products to solve them from Rubbermaid personnel, guest columnists, and blog visitors who comment on blog posts.

If you're looking for a good example of a blog that talks about a company's services, visit the LinkedIn blog at http://blog.linkedin.com. It's a great place to find information about what's happening with the LinkedIn social networking service. That information comes from both LinkedIn customers and from guest authors. Figure 1.6 shows the LinkedIn blog page.

Figure 1.5 *The Adventures in Organization blog, produced by Rubbermaid.*

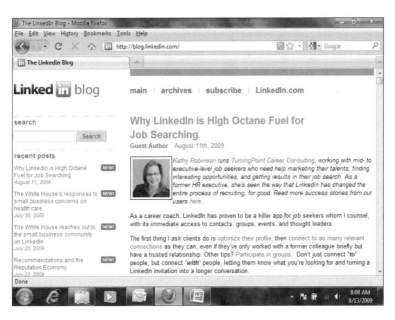

Figure 1.6 *The LinkedIn blog site.*

Reach People

Your business might have many audiences in addition to customers, such as suppliers, vendors, colleagues, and employees. Therefore, before you start writing your blog, identify whom you want to reach with it. You may find that a one-size-fits-all blog that tries to reach all potential audiences is a bad idea. If that's the case, consider maintaining multiple blogs, each dedicated to a specifically identified audience.

For example, you can have a blog on your Web site that's written for your customers. You can have another that lives on your intranet and is for the benefit of your employees. Chapter 3, "Creating a Blogging Strategy," discusses blogging strategies in greater detail, and Chapter 7, "Getting Eyeballs to Your Blog," explains how you get people to read your blog.

What type of blog (or the different types) you create also determines the level of personalization in the blog. For instance, you may want to make your customer blog more personal. After all, you want your customers to "connect" with your products and services, and you certainly want to make people feel that they can trust you. If you have a blog for your internal suppliers, however, you might not want it to be so personal.

You must also decide whether to allow comments on your blog (and if you do allow them, how to manage them). By default, blog sites let readers comment on blog posts, but the blog site owner can turn this feature off. For instance, you might want to have customers comment on your blog posts. In contrast, however, an internal supplier blog might be informational only, with no commenting functionality.

Suppose a blog reader has a question/comment. Most blogging platforms allow you to respond to that question/comment in a message thread that other readers can view. Sometimes people leave inappropriate comments, so you must moderate them. We consider the moderation issue and responsible blogging in Chapter 4, "Blogging Responsibly."

> **Note**
>
> What is a "message thread," anyway? This term refers to a sequence of responses to an initial message posted by someone about a specific topic or discussion. In the case of a blog, when someone comments on an original blog posting, that's the first message in the thread. As you'll learn about later in this book, you can not only comment about an original post but you can also comment about comments you read in a message thread.

Keep Pushing Content

Your faithful blog readers no longer have to go to your blog site to get your latest post (or to see whether you've posted recently). Instead, they can easily set up and use feed readers. Many blogging platforms allow people to receive your new blog posts automatically via the Really Simple Syndication (RSS) method. If you have a program with an RSS reader such as Microsoft Outlook, or if you go on the Web to view RSS feeds such as Google Reader, you can subscribe to your favorite blogs and be alerted when new posts are available. Chapter 2, "Leveraging Other Marketing Tools," tells you more about subscribing to blogs and getting others to subscribe to yours.

> ✉ *Note*
>
> Web designers and marketing people will tell you that you should update your Web site frequently. Their reasoning is that regular updates keep people coming back and search engines are always on the lookout for new content on sites. (If your Web designer or marketing people haven't told you this, perhaps it's time for you to look for new ones.)

Drive People to the Blog

Just because you build it, you can't expect people will come to and comment on your blog. You've got to "say" something. If you can't even think of something to say, what makes you think that others will have anything to add? Therefore, update your blog content at least every few days with new and interesting information about your company specifically or the industry in general. Search engines, especially Google, take particular interest in blog posts because they're updated often and they usually include a lot of the keywords that you want Google to notice in your Web site. If one of your competitors is continually blogging about your industry and you aren't, search engines will find your competitor's blog and place it, not yours, high on the list of search results when someone searches for one or more terms in your industry.

You can also take advantage of other online and offline marketing tools that we discuss in Chapter 2.

Crowdsourcing

Blogs are helpful for keeping in touch with your customers and for finding out who your customers are and what they're thinking about. For example, you can write a post that asks readers where they live, how they use your product, and what improvements they want in your product. They can then answer these questions in the comments.

You can even create a *crowdsourcing* blog. This term refers to asking readers of the blog for feedback so that the business can meet those customers' needs as directly and immediately as possible. The optimal result is that customers will be happier and the business will see greater profit. Starbucks Coffee has done this to great effect with its My Starbucks Idea blog (see Figure 1.7).

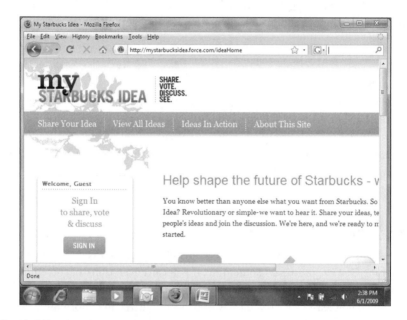

Figure 1.7 *The My Starbucks Idea crowdsourcing blog.*

Starbucks put out the call to its customers both online and through stores to visit the blog site and provide suggestions for making Starbucks better. Visitors can also comment on others' ideas and rate the popularity of the ideas. As of this writing, the number of popular ideas is 9,500. The end result is that Starbucks gets new sources of inspiration from the crowd at little to no cost and the blog invites a more engaged customer base.

Some businesses have been built around crowdsourcing. One example is InnoCentive (http://www.innocentive.com), shown in Figure 1.8. InnoCentive is a company that posts "challenge problems" in a number of areas, from engineering to math to life sciences to business. Their site opens with problems for anyone in the crowd to solve and promises cash prizes to solvers who meet the solution criteria. You can view the various challenges, solutions, and the latest news on the InnoCentive blog.

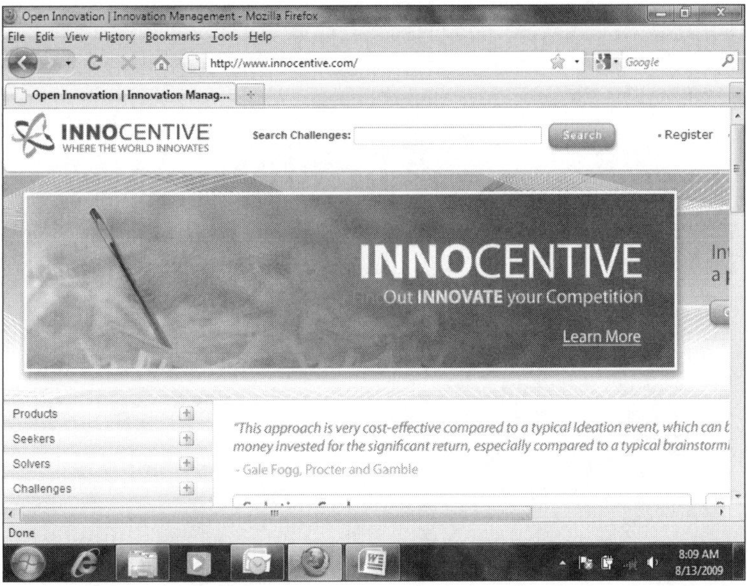

Figure 1.8 *The InnoCentive site.*

The challenge with crowdsourcing is critical mass. You need to get enough people to both respond to you and give you enough feedback that you can act upon. To help meet that challenge, we discuss in Chapter 2 other online and offline marketing tools that you can leverage with your blog.

Case Studies: Intel and Adidas

Like all marketing efforts, there are right ways and wrong ways to do things, and the same is true of blogging. In this section, we look at a more traditional blog from Intel that keeps you posted on the goings on at the chip maker. We also look at a blog that was added to the MySpace social networking site to reach potential customers, but failed to do so.

Intel Inside Scoop Blog

The Intel Inside Scoop blog (http://scoop.intel.com), shown in Figure 1.9, is a good example of a blog that gives you everything you're looking for near the top of the blog (and the first few scroll downs). Having information at or near the top of the blog is important for usability's sake because if your users don't have to scroll down to find information, they will be happier with your blog and more inclined to come back.

Figure 1.9 *The Intel Inside Scoop blog.*

So, why might you want to emulate this blog when you create your own? There are a number of useful features on the blog, including the following:

- A menu at the top of the page takes you to specific sections (for example, bios of the people who write the blog and archives of past blog postings).

- The most recent blog post appears at the top of the page.

- You can readily see where you can subscribe to the blog feed.

- A Recent Posts area links to all the recent posts on the blog home page.

- A Blogroll area links to related blogs. In the case of the Intel Inside Scoop blog, the Blogroll area links to other Intel blogs and other companies' blogs (for example, HP, Dell, and YouTube).

- In a Categories area, readers can view blog posts in areas of their interest.

- Connections link you to other social networking sites. This blog has links to Intel's Twitter, YouTube, and Facebook sites and to pictures on the Flickr photo-sharing site.

Notice that the blog posts on the home page have embedded a variety of information in each one, including text, photos, and videos, such as the Intel LANFest at Intel's Folsom facility, shown in Figure 1.10, which is near where Eric lives.

Figure 1.10 *The Sacramento LANFest 2009 video embedded in a blog post.*

This blog was built with Movable Type, a blogging platform you'll learn about in Chapter 3. However, many of the features on the Intel Inside Scoop blog are also available in other downloadable blog platforms and from hosted services such as WordPress.com.

You can also post blogs on social networking sites to help reach your target audience more directly, but the rules of blogging still apply, such as updating your blog every few days (as the Intel Inside Blog scoop does), so that you don't lose momentum, as we discuss in the next section.

Adidas Soccer MySpace Blog

Adidas serves as our second case study. Adidas, a large multinational shoe company, established a blog on its MySpace site to reach its young customers who frequent MySpace. (Adidas is headquartered in Germany but has its own page, and blog, on MySpace.) Adidas is a good example of the new model for creating brand value, but also proves that even large companies can botch the use of blogs when trying to create that value.

The Momentum Effect

One great online resource for social media marketing examples is the Being Peter Kim Web site (http://www.beingpeterkim.com/2008/09/ive-been-thinki.html). Peter Kim has compiled a number of social media marketing examples and resources.

One of those resources is a presentation that was made in 2007 by Rex Briggs, the CEO of Marketing Evolution. The presentation talks about what Rex calls "the momentum effect" (http://s3.amazonaws.com/thearf-org-aux-assets/downloads/cnc/online-media/2007-10-23_ARF_OM_Briggs_Nagy.pdf). Rex is an avid Adidas fan.

The Briggs presentation discusses the old versus new models of creating value for a brand. You probably know about the business-to-customer (B2C) model of reaching consumers, such as paying for an advertisement in the local paper that will only reach a certain number of people (and hoping it will elicit some business). This is what Briggs calls the old model.

The new model is the customer-to-customer (C2C) model. In this model, each interaction is an impression. People are influenced to visit your community for one or more reasons. For example, a customer may have visited your MySpace page because he or she saw the link in your e-mail newsletter. In the case of Adidas, someone might have done an online search (Google or Yahoo!, for example) for the company and stumbled upon Rex Briggs's profile, and contained in the profile is a link to the Adidas MySpace page.

With each potential customer interaction on the MySpace page as an impression, some of those potential customers pass along what they find to other users. Some of those users will visit your MySpace page and perhaps see more of what your company has to offer, and others won't visit the page but will be positively influenced anyway and pass along the information about Rex Briggs and Adidas to others.

To get the most bang for your buck, the Briggs presentation recommends maximizing both B2C and C2C models. The B2C model requires advertising (such as an advertisement on MySpace) and integration with other offline marketing tools such as magazine advertising, and the C2C model brings people to your profile through links (such as from Rex Briggs's MySpace page to the Adidas MySpace profile), referrals from one person to another, or someone who is self-directed.

So how does one take advantage of the momentum effect? It's all about engaging the customer, and Briggs lists three tips for doing just that:

1. Make your brand a persona so people can identify with you.

2. Make your site (or blog) personal so that you give people a reason to talk about it.

3. Give the consumer a chance to realize a dream or fantasy.

You need to use all three tips to realize the momentum you seek.

Adidas Soccer Losing Momentum

Based on the Briggs report, we decided to visit the Adidas Soccer MySpace profile and see what it offers. The profile, which is shown in Figure 1.11, enables you to create your own photo of yourself with the team you support and its soccer gear (which you then can post on your MySpace page).

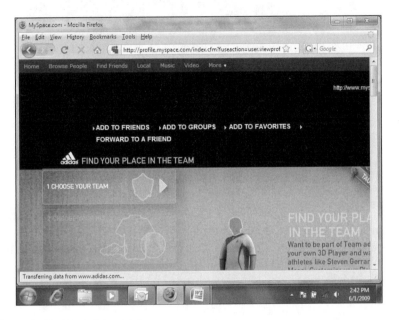

Figure 1.11 *The Adidas MySpace page.*

You can also download desktop wallpaper (that is, an image for your screen background) of your favorite soccer stars, add icons to your desktop (for example, get soccer icons to replace current icons on your desktop), and get product information about the latest shoes (which you can buy online from the Adidas Web site that pops up in a new browser window). You can also add Adidas to your group of friends, leave messages on the forum, view videos, and more.

All these activities give Adidas visitors a chance to tell their stories and interact not only with the company but also with fellow Adidas fans, who in turn spread the word about the Adidas MySpace page and help build the value of the Adidas brand. However, as you scroll down the page, it's easy to overlook the Inside Adidas Soccer section directly below the featured shoes and directly above the Adidas Video Vault.

The Inside Adidas Soccer section is the place for Adidas blog entries, and there is only one entry: Welcome to Inside Adidas Soccer (see Figure 1.12).

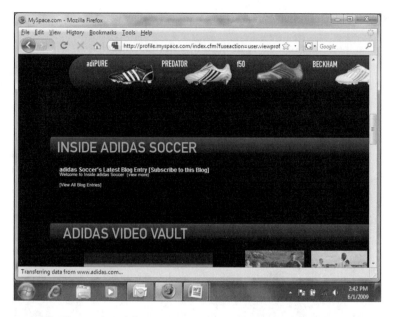

Figure 1.12 *The Inside Adidas Soccer section contains only one blog entry.*

When you click the View More link (or the View All Blog Entries link), the blog page appears as shown in Figure 1.13. There is only one entry, dated Friday, April 25, 2008, which is more than a year ago as of this writing.

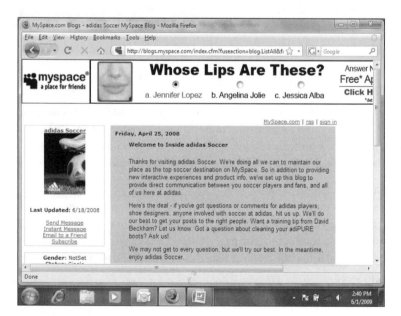

Figure 1.13 *The Inside Adidas Soccer blog page.*

The site states that "we've set up this blog to provide direct communication between you soccer players and fans" because Adidas wants to do "all we can to maintain our place as the top soccer destination on MySpace." The blog invites readers to submit questions or comments for Adidas players and employees, and although 15 readers sent in comments, most between April 26 and July 13, 2008, there have been no responses to these questions or new blog entries posted since the April 25 introductory post.

For a company that has a strong presence on MySpace, the lack of a decent blog is a glaring weakness. What's more, the Adidas Soccer site isn't communicating with its customers as it promised, which makes the site less personal despite what they've done on the main profile page.

Although it's impossible to tell how many people have visited the Adidas blog versus the Intel Inside Scoop blog, the much higher number of comments just on the first page of the Intel Inside Scoop blog suggests that Intel understands blog momentum and Adidas doesn't, and that undercuts Adidas's attempts to market and build its brand online.

Summary

Blogs have been rapidly growing in popularity to the point where blogs are no longer written by a home computer user but also by professional bloggers (those who do so for money) and by businesses that want to get their message out. Businesses use blogs to market their products, keep driving messages to their customers, and get customer feedback.

So how do you leverage your blog to ensure that it's a valuable part of your overall marketing strategy? Let's continue on to Chapter 2.

2

Leveraging Your Blog with Marketing Tools

Blogs are not a panacea for your business challenges. You can't just post a message saying "Hello, world!" or something to that effect on your blog and expect people to come beating down your door. Your blog should complement your other marketing tools to help drive business. For example, if you have a storefront and you want to announce a special sale, you can use the blog to offer a discount to blog readers only (who give the sales clerk a special coupon code found on your blog, for example).

Before you get started with creating a blog for your business, think about two things: creating an integrated marketing toolbox that includes your blog and creating a plan to leverage your blog with those tools to get more business (or at least keep your income at a level that keeps the bills paid).

Today, to have any chance of success, an integrated marketing toolbox must include both "online" and "offline" components. You must have an online presence (one that you're actually proud of) to come across as credible, even when you attend a networking event sponsored by your local chamber of commerce or give a potential client your business card. You also can't have all of your marketing efforts online and expect people to automatically find you that way. On a regular basis, you need to get out of your office and get out and talk to your existing and potential customers. Online marketing, even video-based marketing, is somewhat impersonal and is no substitute for face-to-face conversations. Customers look for a personal connection with a business owner, and if they can't get it from you, they'll look to your competition.

Online Marketing

Blogs can mesh with your other online marketing efforts (for example, your Web site, e-mail marketing, and your efforts to promote your business on social networking sites). These efforts must be as consistent as possible to ensure that you constantly reinforce your brand. In this section, we talk about the various online marketing tools and how you can use them in tandem with blogs.

Web Site

Your online marketing efforts start with your Web site. About 10 years ago, having a Web site was seen as a luxury. Today, it's a necessity if you're going to be taken seriously by potential customers, competitors, and your industry. And if you expect your Web site to actually bring you business, it can't just be a placeholder or a brochure. Your site must actively engage visitors by including interesting content, and you must update the site regularly with new information to keep people coming back (as shown by the case study later in this chapter).

E-Mail Marketing

Your online marketing efforts have to be part of a system that includes other related marketing efforts, and they require you to have some skin in the game. That is, you need to budget both time and money to your online efforts, and those efforts go beyond setting up a Web site. After you have a Web site, you need to initiate a regular e-mail marketing campaign so that you can continue to drive interest to your Web site, keep in touch with your customers, and give them an incentive to stay involved with you, such as regular coupons or special events.

Plenty of e-mail marketing solutions are available online that don't cost a lot of money. You can view a list of the more popular e-mail marketing services on the Email Marketing Software Comparison Web site at www.email-marketing-options.com (see Figure 2.1). Many of them allow you to set the timing of your campaigns, such as when to send them out, and they also let you customize the look of your newsletter.

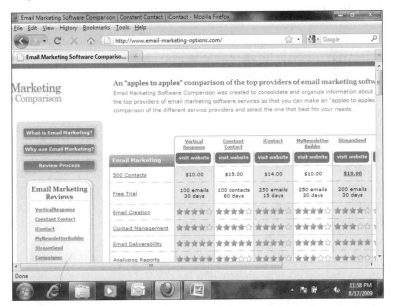

Figure 2.1   *The Email Marketing Software Comparison Web site.*

More Work... and Potential Solutions

In today's Web 2.0 world, you also need to

- Have a blog so that you can continue to drive people to your online presence. You also need to moderate and respond to comments made to your blog posts (if you allow comments on your blog).

- Be involved in social networking Web sites.

- Go to related sites, including those belonging to your industry and your competitors, so that you can stay current with what's going on.

When you add it all up, there's a lot of work to do to keep your online marketing system running, and some businesses cringe when they learn must budget for their online marketing initiatives just as they budget their time, money, and personnel for other marketing programs. Businesses often want to know how much time it takes. But, of course, that depends on what you want to do.

Larger businesses often hire someone full time to manage their online marketing efforts. (Sites such as Dice.com have job posting for occupations with titles such as "online marketing specialist.") Smaller businesses and nonprofits have other possibilities: They can hire a part-time assistant to handle the tasks discussed in this section, or they can pick and choose what tools to use.

A Part-Time Assistant

You can offload a number of tasks onto a part-time assistant tasked with updating your current status on blogs and social networking sites. You might have to spend only 10 minutes or so talking with your assistant about what's happening. The assistant can then do the work from a home computer at a minimal charge.

Tip

Local chambers of commerce are a great way to find virtual assistant companies that offer small business owners flexible options for helping them take care of daily tasks for a small fee (including updating social networking sites). Through your networking, you may learn about "freelancers" who are interested in working from home part time on a flexible schedule. You may also want to check out your local colleges to see whether they offer internships. If so, you can provide students with the valuable experience of learning social marketing aspects of a business at little to no charge.

You may want to write a rough draft or an outline for your assistant to follow (and you may want to do the same for blog entries you write). Although you may task your assistant with writing the final copy, only you can tell your customers what you think they need to know. (This doesn't apply, of course, if your assistant can read your mind.)

The one thing that your assistant may not be able to do (or not be able to do without significant training) is respond to comments made to your blog posts. You might need to do most of the replying yourself, at least at first. You can help steer your respondents and make your life (and your assistant's) easier by giving them clear guidelines for leaving comments and encouraging your blogging community to police themselves. We discuss how the *Sacramento Bee* newspaper does this in one of our case studies later in this chapter.

Pick and Choose the Tools to Use

Fortunately, you don't have to use every tool in the toolbox we've mentioned in this chapter if you don't have the manpower/cash to get everything you want right away. Here are some tips to help you get the most out of your time and money when it comes to online marketing:

- Use the Ping.fm Web service (http://ping.fm) shown in Figure 2.2 to quickly update your status on social networking sites and blogs. After you set up the blogs and social networking sites, you need to update in Ping.fm. To update all of them, you just log in to Ping.fm, type your updated status, and submit it. Then Ping.fm forwards your updated status to those sites and saves you quite a bit of time.

Figure 2.2   *The Ping.fm Web site.*

- If you can't afford to have someone create a Web site for you (and you don't have the personnel to do this yourself), you can create a blog and have that act as your Web site. If you want to have your own URL, talk with your Internet service provider about having your Web site index page point directly to the blog home page. To view an example of a blog as a Web site, visit the Waterside Productions Web site, which is our literary agency, at http://www.watersidesyndication.com (see Figure 2.3).

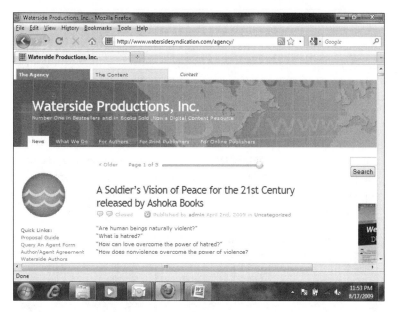

Figure 2.3   *The Waterside Productions Web site.*

- Take advantage of free e-mail marketing trials. Many e-mail marketing firms offer free trials so that you can see how their systems work before you decide whether you want to pay for them. For example, Constant Contact, which is one of the more popular e-mail marketing solutions available, offers a 60-day free trial for new members, as shown in Figure 2.4.

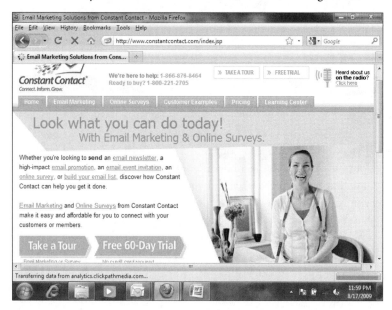

Figure 2.4   *The Constant Contact free 60-day trial offer button.*

- Add Google Alerts so that you can get e-mail updates in the topics of interest to you. If you were to try to go through all the Web sites to glean information from the Web, you'd never do anything productive. Google Alerts checks the Web for you based on the topics you select and then sends a digest e-mail to you with links to the full articles. When you visit Google Analytics at www.google.com/analytics (see Figure 2.5), you can select your search terms, how to search, and where to send the results. If you already have a Google account, you can sign in to manage your alerts.

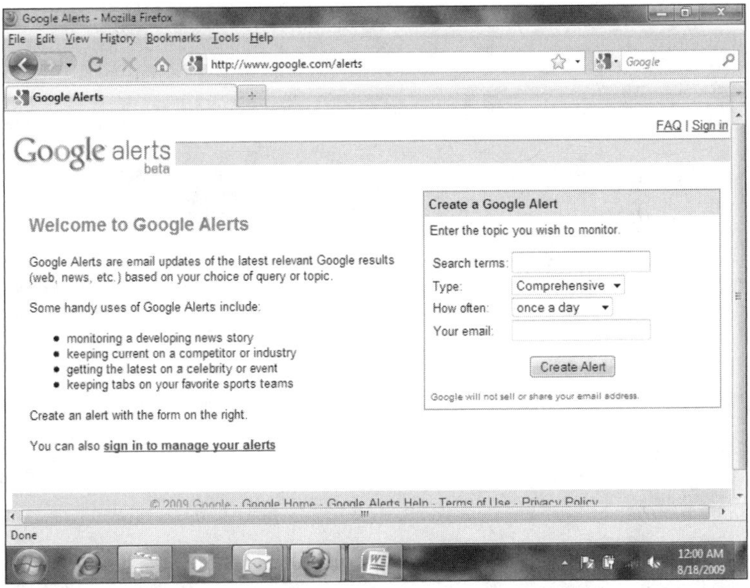

Figure 2.5   *The Google Analytics Web site.*

Offline Marketing

Offline marketing is the traditional marketing that your customers may still expect you to engage in to get their business. *Traditional marketing* refers to getting out and networking in person, perhaps advertising in print/radio/television or perhaps going out to a local or area trade show to promote your business.

Although you might need to leverage some types of traditional advertising because your market research has determined that your customer base is more receptive to such, you may still want to be on the cutting edge when it comes to marketing to bring in other types of clients. For example, your older clients may prefer printed materials, such as direct mail delivered directly to their offices. Younger recipients may not only view such direct mail as ineffective but also wasteful. Or you might

decide to network at chamber of commerce luncheons rather than young professionals' organizations because you have a better chance of finding solid leads at
those events.

So how can your blog help you determine whether any offline marketing strategies
are right for your business? The blog can both inform customers about what you're
doing to gain their business and ask for feedback. One recent blog we viewed was
on Frogloop (www.frogloop.com), shown in Figure 2.6. That blog sparked a debate
about whether direct mail was dying or already dead in light of the popularity of
blogs and social media sites.

Figure 2.6   *The Frogloop blog post about the future of direct mail.*

Various conversations like the one on Frogloop are taking place on the Web. (Just
search for "direct mail advertising blog" on your favorite search engine.) If you start
a conversation about your marketing practices and ideas on your blog with your
customers, you'll most likely get some valuable information that will help you
determine which offline marketing strategies you should employ, if any. You may
also get some ideas for new blog posts and new conversations.

▶ *Caution*

Timing is also important when you write blog posts about something you
find interesting. For example, about a year ago, I attended a chamber of
commerce presentation by a fellow chamber member. The following day, I
produced my biweekly newsletter and included a critique of the member's

presentation. She immediately e-mailed me when she received my e-mail, expressing her embarrassment at my critique because several people on my mailing list were also chamber members and knew her (and could recognize I was referring to her in my critique).

Another problem can be that search engines can pick up text in a blog that the writer doesn't want people to see. Such an unfortunate occurrence happened to the Poor Richard's Almanac blog in 2008. Google decided not to use the first sentence of the blog post in the search results, but instead used a sentence that the author carefully buried so as to turn the search result from a PG rating to an NC-17. You can read more about the episode on the Poor Richard's Almanac blog at http://ourfriendben.wordpress.com/2008/05/02/how-humiliating.

Pushing Information via RSS

Okay, so is there anything about online marketing that actually makes things easier for you? Well, perhaps not for you, but certainly for your readers. You can set up your blog so that your customers can subscribe to your blog feed using RSS technology. RSS is an acronym for Really Simple Syndication, and there are many different applications for reading RSS feeds, from software applications like Microsoft Outlook to Web apps such as Bloglines (see Figure 2.7). These sites not only let people subscribe to blogs but also categorize them (and the case of Bloglines, it puts all your RSS feeds on one home page).

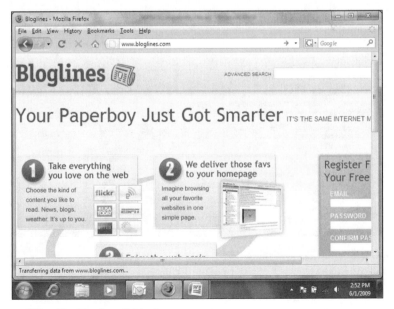

Figure 2.7   *The Bloglines Web site.*

You create your own Bloglines account with a unique username and password, and then you can search for blogs that you want to add or you can add blogs from the Bloglines top 1,000 list of blogs. As you read the blogs, you can click the Discuss link underneath the post if comments are accepted for that post and Bloglines will take you directly to the blog so that you can read other comments and add a comment of your own.

Many blogging platforms that we discuss in Chapter 3, "Creating a Blogging Strategy," enable you to add RSS subscriptions for your readers. RSS subscriptions let users receive your new blog posts automatically either within a newsreader program (like Microsoft Outlook) or within an online newsreader (like Google Reader). The first time the user reads the blog, the user can click the orange RSS icon either on the blog page or in the browser address bar to subscribe to that blog feed.

The orange RSS icon is the easy way to add an RSS feed to your preferred newsreader program. Just click the icon, and your browser will ask you where you want to read the feed. For example, the Being Peter Kim site shown in Figure 2.8 talks about social networking, Web 2.0 technologies, and more. The RSS icon appears in the upper-right corner of the page.

RSS icon

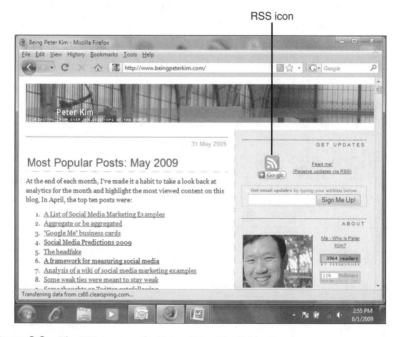

Figure 2.8 *The RSS icon on the Being Peter Kim Web site.*

The benefit of an RSS feed is that you can push information to your clients repeatedly, which gives you an opportunity to keep them coming back to your business. For example, you could give subscribers to your blog special offers that no one else can get.

Getting Customers to Subscribe

So how do you get your customers to subscribe to your blog after they've discovered it? You can employ a number of simple strategies to encourage customers to read your blog:

- Put an invitation to read your blog (and a link to the blog site) in a conspicuous location on every page of your Web site.

- Put a link to your blog and an invitation in your e-mail newsletter.

- Share the blog entry on other social networking sites such as Digg, LinkedIn, and Facebook. Most social networking sites, including the ones listed here, connect directly to blogs, and you'll learn more about that in Chapter 3.

- If you have an audio/video podcast as well as a blog, be sure to mention your blog in each broadcast.

- If you have several different blogs, ensure that each blog links to the other.

Taking Care of Your Readers

After you get a list of your readers, it's important to keep them interested by sharing quality information often. Here are some pointers for taking care of your blog readership:

- As mentioned earlier in this chapter, it's always good to keep on top of what's going on both online and offline to try to find recent topics to write about and share with your audience.

- Readers expect to read information written in your voice, not someone else's. So if you're going to lift quotes from another blog or another source, be sure that it's properly quoted and referenced.

- Your blog is a reflection on you and your company.

- Your blog is going to stick around in the Internet ether for a long time. Be sure that what you say has value.

- If you're not sure about any of the previous points after you finish writing a blog entry, run it by a trusted friend, colleague, or business mentor. A fresh set of eyes can give you the insight you lack because you're too close to the material.

- Consider enabling your readers to leave comments about your entries. The more involved your readers are, the more likely they will be to come back to your blog and to your site. However, there are some caveats that are discussed in the next section and in Chapter 4, "Blogging Responsibly."

- Consider sending a survey to your readers through a survey Web site such as Constant Contact or SurveyMonkey.com to find out what they think about your blog and your other marketing efforts so that you can make it better.

We go into more detail about these tips in later chapters.

Case Studies

Having plenty of information in your blogs is a great way to keep your readers interested and coming back for more, and the city of Arvada, Colorado, has a Web site that is a good example of that. Our second case study looks at the *Sacramento Bee* newspaper and how they have created appropriate text to advise those who comment about the rules of civility in the online forums.

City of Arvada

The city of Arvada, which is west of Denver in the metropolitan area, has a good example of a Web site (shown in Figure 2.9) that links to its related social networking sites, including Twitter, Facebook, and YouTube.

The city of Arvada site contains a number of videos about city goings-on, pictures of the city, and even a blog about the Arvada Center for the Arts and Humanities, shown in Figure 2.10, which includes information about upcoming events. The blog and other Web site information are updated regularly so that people who live in the area (and especially tourists) can learn more about the area and plan ahead.

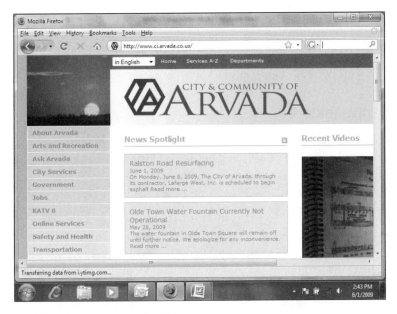

Figure 2.9   *The City of Arvada Web site.*

Figure 2.10   *The Arvada Center for the Arts and Humanities blog.*

For the most part, the information on the City of Arvada Web site is easy to find, but be warned that it's easy to bury your blog in your site. The Arvada Center blog was not easy for us to find. We had to click four times to get to the blog, and the blog was actually on a separate Web site for the Arvada Center that is linked to the city site. In our humble opinion, a single Web link from the city home page to the blog would make it easier for citizens and tourists alike to get information about arts in the community.

The Sacramento Bee

Should you invite comments on your Web site? Although the usual answer is yes, because you have control over your blog, it's also true that you don't have control over the people who make comments on your site. Therefore, as mentioned earlier in this chapter, it's a good idea to tell people the rules of the road as often as possible.

One category of blog sites where it's good to state the rules of the commenting road is newspaper blogs. In the past, people wrote letters to the editor, but that was less immediate, and because of space constraints, few people had their letters printed. Today, people can log on to a newspaper Web site when they find something in the paper they like or dislike, scroll to the bottom of the story, and leave a comment.

The *Sacramento Bee* is one such newspaper. The *Bee* Web site shown in Figure 2.11 is like many newspaper sites in that it produces articles about controversial topics every day. For people in Sacramento, that includes the Sacramento Kings professional basketball team and Proposition 8, the proposition to amend the California Constitution to define marriage as between a man and a woman.

Figure 2.11   *The Sacramento Bee Web site.*

At the bottom of each article is a section titled About Comments, shown in Figure 2.12. The section is a disclaimer telling people about the basics of their commenting policy. It also states that "flagrant or repeat violators will be banned." Before someone can leave a comment, the user must log in to the *Bee*'s Web site. If the user is a flagrant or repeat violator, *Bee* moderators will tag the user account as a violator. When the violating user logs in again, the site will inform the user that comments are disabled because of those violations.

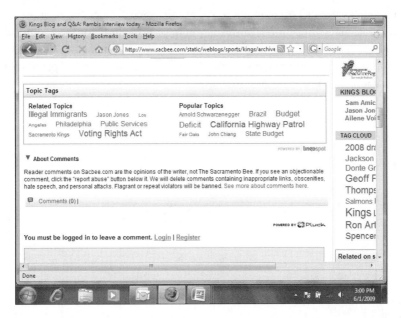

Figure 2.12   *The Sacramento Bee Web site About Comments section.*

Readers can learn more by clicking the See More about Comments Here link at the end of the paragraph. When the user clicks the link, text appears below the first paragraph with more specific information about do's and don'ts, including "do not attack other users," "stay on topic," and "do not repeat the same comment over and over."

This information makes it clearer to the reader that the *Bee* doesn't screen comments; instead, it relies on readers reporting abuse. Readers just click the Report Abuse button after an entry they think warrants a review by the moderator, and the moderator of the *Bee* site can then determine whether the comment is abusive/inappropriate. If so, the post is deleted, and the moderator takes appropriate action against the abuser. However, the *Bee*'s moderation policies also make clear that they are the sole arbiter of what is appropriate and what isn't on their site.

The moral of the story with the *Bee*'s blog is that the same is true of your blog. What is posted on your blog, including comments, will reflect on your company, so be sure to add information about responsible commenting to your blog if at all possible. You'll learn more about responsible blogging in Chapter 4.

Summary

Although blogs aren't the solution to your business challenges, they can mesh with your other marketing efforts. However, you must plan ahead for the additional workload that a blog brings and also ensure that all your marketing efforts are consistent so you constantly reinforce your brand. Let's move on to Chapter 3 to learn more about creating a blogging strategy.

3

Creating a Blogging Strategy

When you decide to create a blog for your business, finding out where to start can be a bit overwhelming. There are plenty of blogging platforms for you to choose from that are hosted by companies on Web sites or are available for you to download, customize, and host on your own Web site.

Discovering the right blogging platform for you has to be the first part of a holistic blogging strategy. In this instance, **holistic** means that you consider the entire whole of your strategy rather than individual parts. For example, you can have people subscribe to your blog and send updates automatically and in real time through a RSS (Really Simple Syndication) feed. You'll also want to connect your blog to your Web site so that people who visit your blog will be compelled to visit your Web site to learn more about you (and vice versa). These are all parts in a larger, holistic strategy of driving readers to your blog and making it as easy as possible for your readers to find and read your blog.

*You should also have a profile on social networking sites and a link to your blog on that profile. In these ways, you can establish **thought leadership** or **mind share**. You might have heard these terms in reference to companies such as Apple and Sony, which don't have a lot of market share but the media is always talking about these companies anyway. Blogs help you gain mind share, and because of that mind share, others will recognize you and your company as an expert in your field. This eventually leads to more interest and more business for your company.*

This chapter begins with a review of blogging platforms. If you already know what platform to use, you can skip the next section and move ahead to "Finding the Blog Best for Your Business."

Blogging Platforms

You can produce your blog in one of two ways. You can host your blog for free on a site that lets anyone create a blog using a set of stock templates (or an HTML template if you want to have your own look). These sites include the name of the blogging site in the URL, such as http://zenoferox.blogspot.com, which is the Web site for the Zeno Ferox blog site on Blogger that we referenced in Chapter 1, "Why Are Blogs So Important?" If you want a blog to be on your own site, you can download software that you can install on your Web server and configure it. Some download options are free, but others are not, depending on the features you want on your blog.

If you want to start blogging quickly and get your name out there right away, hosting your blog on a blogging site is the best way to go. The following sections discuss some of the more popular blogging sites.

WordPress.com

WordPress started as open source software for people to publish blogs on their own Web sites in 2003, but in 2005, WordPress decided to host its own blogs for the Web public at www.wordpress.com, which is shown in Figure 3.1 (http://en.wikipedia.org/wiki/Wordpress.com).

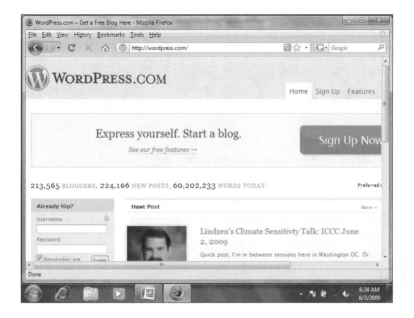

Figure 3.1   *The WordPress.com Web site.*

You might notice that we used WordPress instead of WordPress.com. That's because there are two separate WordPress sites: one with the address www.wordpress.com and another with the address www.wordpress.org. The difference between the two is that the WordPress.com site hosts blogs on its site—all you have to do is go through a few steps to create your blog.

WordPress.org, on the other hand, is a site shown in Figure 3.2 that lets you download the WordPress blogging system so that you can install it on your server, configure it, and then post blog entries.

The difference is that on WordPress.com you create your blog from a set of stock templates as discussed earlier in this chapter and the URL has *wordpress.com* in it. With WordPress.org, you download and configure the WordPress system so that you can have greater control over how the blog looks and have a custom URL.

Is the WordPress site best for your blog? And if that's true, should you use WordPress.com or WordPress.org?

To answer the first question, WordPress is a popular blogging system, and its blogs are rated highly by Google and other major search engines. The downside is that you have the Wordpress.com site name in the URL, so your blog won't look like it comes from your business. Unless you pay for WordPress premium features, your readers will occasionally see Google text ads on your blog (which help WordPress offer free accounts).

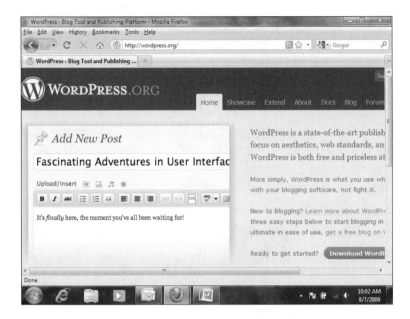

Figure 3.2 *The WordPress.org Web site.*

You can download the WordPress system free from WordPress.org. You just need the open source Web language PHP and open source database MySQL installed to install it. WordPress is customizable, and despite the fact that WordPress provides excellent instructions for setting up a system (and even suggests offering hosting services if you need them), it will take time for your team to get a blog up and running.

If you've got the manpower to create a blog and branding its URL under your own name is important to you, consider downloading and using WordPress to power your blog.

TypePad

Like WordPress, Six Apart's TypePad sprouted from the company's blog publishing software, Movable Type. Like WordPress, TypePad is a blog that is hosted on its site.

TypePad, shown in Figure 3.3, has become a popular paid service that many mainstream media companies use, including ABC, MSNBC, the BBC, and Sky News (http://en.wikipedia.org/wiki/TypePad). TypePad prides itself on being a full-service blogging site that's also reasonably priced; as of this writing, the Basic plan costs $4.95 per month, and TypePad offers four other plans up to Business Class at $89.95 per month per blog.

Figure 3.3   *The TypePad Web site.*

So why do businesses use TypePad? According to the TypePad site, you can do a lot of things in TypePad that you either can't do in Blogger or WordPress or that cost extra in WordPress. For example, you can password-protect your blog, which costs extra in WordPress. However, the blog platforms are constantly improving. So, what some sites tell you is an advantage really isn't. For example, the TypePad site's comparison page states that TypePad easily connects to your social networking profiles, but recently WordPress and LinkedIn (as well as other sites) have become much more proficient at connecting with each other. So, do your research.

Speaking of research, TypePad does give you a free 14-day trial so that you can learn whether it is right for you. If you like it, you can view the TypePad pricing page to determine what features you need in your blog that correspond to the plan TypePad offers.

Vox

If you don't want to pay for TypePad, Six Apart offers the free Vox blogging service shown in Figure 3.4. The Vox service prides itself on letting users create blogs more quickly using different features (including audio and video), add new blog posts quickly, and send blogs only to specific groups. These groups can be the entire world, your family/friends, or you only. By "friends," we mean someone you've identified as a trusted person who's also a Vox user. (If you're familiar with friends on Facebook or other social networking sites, Vox works in the same way.)

Figure 3.4   *The Vox Web site.*

Only people who can view your blog post can comment on it. For example, if you write a blog post that only your friends can view, only your friends can comment on your post. Keep this in mind if you want to test Vox as a blogging platform.

Blogger

Blogger, shown in Figure 3.5, was created in 2000 by Pyra Labs, and was one of the earliest blog publishing systems available on the Web (http://en.wikipedia.org/wiki/Blogger_(service)). Blogger's popularity got the attention of Google, which bought Pyra Labs in 2003, and Google's increased popularity over the years has resulted in more popularity for Blogger. What's more, the connectivity between Blogger and Google place Blogger blogs higher in Google search results, and that's one good reason for your business to consider Blogger.

Figure 3.5   *The Blogger Web site.*

LiveJournal

LiveJournal, shown in Figure 3.6, claims on its Web site that it is a "community publishing platform" that combines blogging and a social network. Like MySpace and some other social networking sites, you can add and connect to other "friends" in the system. Like Vox, only people who can view your blog post can comment on it. So if your post is only visible to your friends, only your friends can comment.

Figure 3.6 *The LiveJournal Web site.*

Blog Software

You might decide that you want your own Web server to host your blog, to keep all your pages under the same URL (your Web site address). For example, if you have a Web site called www.nancysnursery.com, you might want the blog to have the URL blog.nancysnursery.com rather than something like nancysnursery.wordpress.com. You might also want to have a blog development platform so that you can customize it to your needs. A number of free and commercial blog packages are available, some of which are offered by companies that also host their own Web-based blogs for others to use. We'll take a brief tour of some of these sites, starting with the free blogging systems.

TypePad, WordPress, and LiveJournal all have their own server software that you can download from their sites for free, but the LiveJournal and WordPress blog systems have different names. LiveJournal lets you download its server code from its Web site for free. If you want to download the WordPress platform, you have to visit http://www.wordpress.org and download the application from the download page, as shown in Figure 3.7.

Figure 3.7   *The WordPress.org Web site download page.*

The downloadable version of TypePad is called Movable Type. You can download the Movable Type Developer or Movable Type Pro Blogger versions of Movable Type for free, as shown in Figure 3.8. However, if you want even more functionality, you must download the Business or Enterprise versions and pay for those services.

Figure 3.8   *The Movable Type Web site.*

A couple of other interesting free blogging applications take a somewhat different approach. Thingamablog, with the Web site shown in Figure 3.9, doesn't require a third-party host, and it doesn't require you to configure any programming languages or a database to get your blog up and running. You need the Java programming language installed on your computer (available free from Oracle), and all you have to do is install the Thingamablog application to your computer and go through the installation procedure.

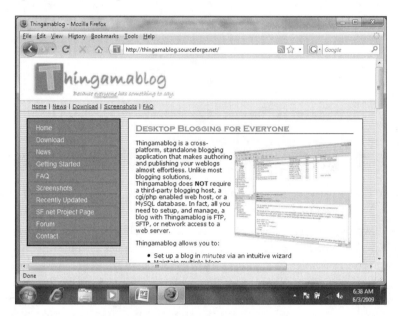

Figure 3.9 *The Thingamablog Web site.*

Drupal goes even further: It's a flexible content management system that can be modified for a number of requirements. As the Drupal Web site's About page explains, there are a number of applications for the free Drupal system, from discussion Web sites to e-commerce applications to social networking Web sites (see Figure 3.10).

Figure 3.10   *The Drupal Web site About page.*

Finding the Blog Best for Your Business

In the beginning, there was the text blog, and it was good. As blogging became more popular and multimedia objects exploded on the Web, blogging sites and software kept up and eventually created different types of blogging that fall into many different categories.

Vlogs

Vlogs, which is a conflation of *video blogs*, include video clips that you can view in the blog. Some sites, such as YouTube, let you post videos on their site for others to view. Blogging sites also let you import video objects into blog posts. Some blogs, like the Bleeding Edge TV blog shown in Figure 3.11, also let you download the video so that you can see the latest and greatest tech gadgets offline.

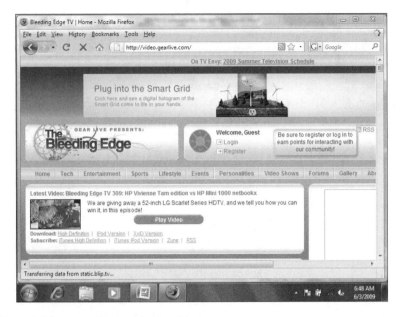

Figure 3.11   *The Bleeding Edge TV blog.*

For example, Nancy's Lullaby Nursery (mentioned earlier in this chapter) started off with a text blog about infant and toddler care. But Nancy, the owner, decided that she wanted to put together a video showing some care techniques. Her husband recorded the video for the blog, edited the blog on his computer, saved the file in the appropriate format for the blog, and posted the video along with a little text in a new blog post. To avoid any permission issues with putting photos and videos of babies on their blog, Nancy uses several different sized dummies in her examples.

Photoblogs

Photoblogs are self-explanatory: They are blogs that use photos as their primary means of communication. Kathleen Connally's photoblog of Durham Township, Pennsylvania, shown in Figure 3.12, won the 2007 Best American Photoblog (www.photobloggies.org).

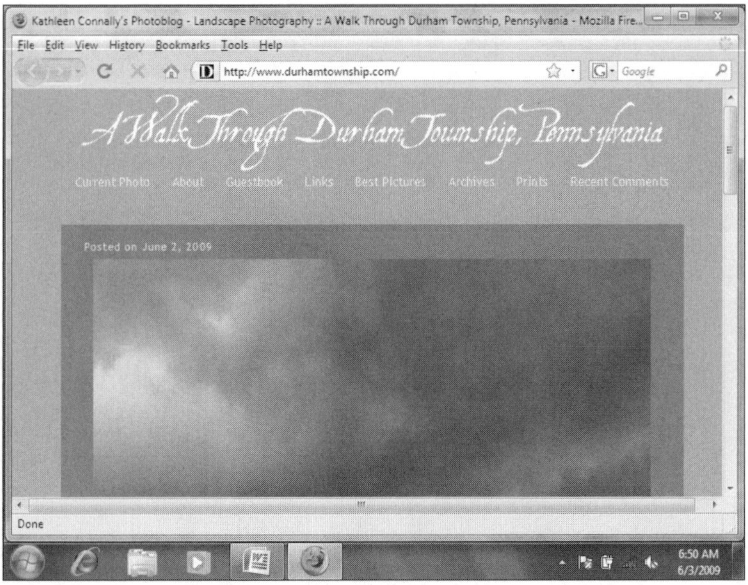

Figure 3.12   *The Kathleen Connally photoblog.*

In the case of Nancy's Lullaby Nursery, Nancy decided she wanted to take pictures of babies that had "graduated" from her program. (Nancy cares for babies and toddlers only up to 18 months of age.) So, Nancy put her husband to work again and had him take pictures of her with happy toddlers upon their "graduation." She then added them to the latest blog post.

Podcast Blogs

Soon after Apple's iPod became a sensation, people learned how to record audio files and have them download onto iPods for listening. Thus, the term *podcasting* was coined. Today, the New Oxford American Dictionary defines podcasting as "a digital recording of a radio broadcast or similar program, made available on the Internet for downloading to a personal audio player." As newer iPod models became capable of displaying videos, and blogs were able to do that, the definition of a podcast expanded to include video as well. The This Week in Tech blog produced by Leo Laporte, as shown in Figure 3.13, is an example of a blog with an audio podcast in MP3 format.

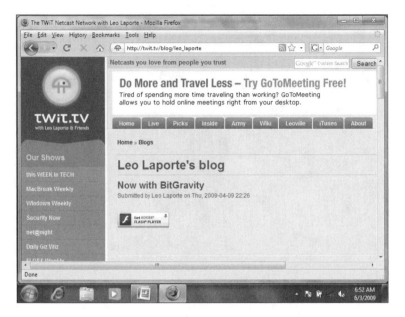

Figure 3.13   *The This Week in Tech blog with podcast.*

For Nancy's Lullaby Nursery, she found that she was starting to become a trusted resource and people began asking her for more information. She decided to entice people to receive an e-mail newsletter by offering access to a members' area of her Web site that included free podcasts that she recorded using her husband's computer, headset, and the free, open source Audacity sound recorder. Podcast topics Nancy has talked about include how to calm a teething baby, when to feed your baby different types of foods, and how to select the right daycare provider. Nancy also made the latter podcast available to the public on her Web site so interested customers could hear Nancy talk about finding the right provider.

Tumblelogs

The term *tumblelog* describes a blog that includes a wide variety of blogging types, such as video, audio, and photos, along with text. The Projectionist blog shown in Figure 3.14 is a good example of a tumblelog.

Figure 3.14   *The Projectionist tumblelog.*

As you can tell from the figure, tumblelogs are primarily lighter on text and heavier on multimedia elements such as photos and video. Usually the text describes the photo or video shown in the tumblelog. In the case of Nancy's Lullaby Nursery, the addition of videos and photos has turned her blog into a tumblelog, and as her blog has become more popular with the addition of multimedia elements, she's focused on that more than writing text.

Microblogs

A recent trend in blogging is called microblogging, where people don't have to type much to communicate. Indeed, microblogging sites such as Twitter only let you post 140 characters in each blog post, so you must be brief. Eric's Twitter site, shown in Figure 3.15, has a lot of updates from people he follows on Twitter.

A related feature of microblogging is sideblogging, where you can post little snippets of information that don't require a lot of thought. For example, in the Alex King blog shown in Figure 3.16, the information in the Twittering section is considered a sideblog because it is little snippets of information presented as bullet points. Sideblogs have become so popular on blog sites that you can add your own sideblog widgets on blogging platform sites such as WordPress.

Figure 3.15 *Eric Butow's Twitter page.*

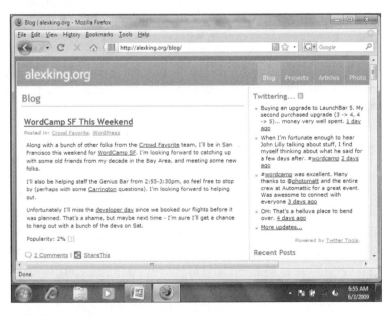

Figure 3.16 *Sideblogs on the Alex King blog.*

Moblogs

As cell phones and PDAs started merging into complete communications devices
with which you could talk to people, get your e-mail, listen to music, and surf the
Web, blogging sites such as SingTel's Moblog (mobile log = mblog) made it easy for
people to upload text and photos to their blog. People can then log on to the
Moblog Web site, as shown in Figure 3.17, and view your latest photos.

Figure 3.17   *The Moblog Web site.*

Tip

If you're not sure where to start, the plethora of blogging options to choose
from can seem rather daunting. The best thing to do in this case is to just
go back to the basics and listen to your customers. If you ask them where
they congregate online, how they do so, and what information they'd like
from you, you'll have a better idea of how to build your blog. For example,
if your clients tell you they primarily use their smartphones to travel and
share information, you might want to create a moblog to invite your customers to upload their photos and videos from their smartphones to share
with other blog readers. You may also want to include videos in your blog,
such as showing people how a new product works. It's all part of responsible blogging that you'll learn about in Chapter 4, "Blogging Responsibly."

Combining Blogs with Other Networking Sites

Your business may want to participate in a number of other social networking sites. For example, if you market one or more products to people in the 18 to 29 age range, you might be interested in marketing on social networking sites such as MySpace, Facebook, and Twitter. If you market products/services to the business community, LinkedIn may be the site you target instead.

Social networking and blogging sites have become much tighter in the past year, and now it's easy for you to post a new blog entry and have it post on all your social networking sites so that viewers can read it and also link back to your blog and Web site. MySpace, Facebook, Twitter, and LinkedIn are the big-four social networking sites when it comes to businesses trying to get in front of their customers, so we'll focus on how to combine blogs with those sites in this section.

MySpace

The first Web site that sparked the social networking craze in the early 2000s was MySpace. Teenagers and young adults discovered the site first as a means to connect with each other, and later, adults discovered the value in connecting with others through MySpace. Although MySpace was the most popular social networking site for several years, Facebook has recently surpassed MySpace's growth and total user numbers. Even so, MySpace maintains a strong following.

MySpace was an early adopter of combining a blog in its social networking system, and you can easily add a blog to your MySpace profile. For example, Figure 3.18 shows the blog entry page within Eric's MySpace page. Over the years, as MySpace has tried to keep up with its competitors, the system has added the capability of adding audio and video files to MySpace profiles that act as audio blogs and vlogs, respectively.

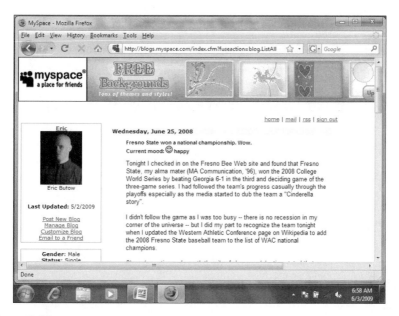

Figure 3.18   *Eric Butow's MySpace blog page.*

Facebook

Facebook was originally popular with college students who didn't want to deal with the younger crowd on MySpace and preferred Facebook's cleaner interface. Eventually, more users of all ages and from many countries worldwide came to Facebook to make it the largest social networking site in the world as of this writing.

Both Facebook and LinkedIn have built-in applications for you to link your blog, which is either hosted on a Web site or hosted on your own server, to your Facebook or LinkedIn profiles so that you can update simultaneously to all your blogging sites.

It takes some doing to get to the list of Facebook blog applications for you to review. In the lower-left corner of the page, click Applications, Browse More Applications. In the Search box near the top of the page, type **blog** and then press Enter. You'll see the first of four pages of search results with blog applications you can use (see Figure 3.19). Each blog application has different features and ratings, so you can choose the application that's right for you.

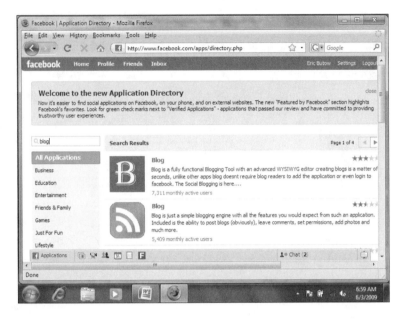

Figure 3.19 *Page I of the list of blog applications on Facebook.*

LinkedIn

LinkedIn launched in 2003 as a social networking site designed solely for business professionals. The site has continued to grow in popularity because it's not only a place for business people to connect, but also for people to search for jobs and for recruiters to find potential job candidates.

LinkedIn introduced its suite of applications in 2008, and one of them is a direct link between your WordPress blog and LinkedIn. Open the Applications in the LinkedIn home page by clicking the Applications link in the left-side navigation bar. You'll see two blog applications, as shown in Figure 3.20.

One is for linking your blog on the WordPress.com site, and the other, Blog Link, connects not only your WordPress.com blog but also any blogging platform produced by Six Apart (WordPress.org, Vox, TypePad, and Movable Type) and to other blogging platforms such as Blogger and LiveJournal.

Figure 3.20   *The LinkedIn Applications page with the WordPress and Blog Link applications.*

Twitter

The Twitter Web site is the most popular Web site in the microblogging category. Twitter lets you send microblogs, or "tweets," of 140 characters or less to your Twitter friends. You can also add cross-reference tags to a specific topic so that you can see all tweets from all Twitter users that are related to that topic.

At the bottom of the Twitter home page is an Apps link. When you click that link, you can view several popular Twitter applications developed by third-party companies. You can also view a list of many other applications, but the problem is that this list is too long and it's very hard to find blogging applications short of searching for the word *blog* in your browser.

To avoid undue hassle, head to the twitterfeed site shown in Figure 3.21 (www.twitterfeed.com). This site checks your blog for new feeds at an interval you specify and then posts the information to your Twitter feed so that your followers can click the blog link and read your latest posts.

Figure 3.21   The twitterfeed Web site.

Case Studies

It's easy to integrate blogs and social networking sites together because the various sites make it easy. However, social networks are not the only way to push people to read your blog. Your Web site also needs to integrate your different blogs and social networking sites. This isn't only important, it's vital.

Okay, so how do you go about it? Let's take a couple of examples from the real world and see what *BusinessWeek* magazine and KCBS radio in San Francisco are doing to stay connected online with their readership.

BusinessWeek

It's not news that the print media isn't doing well, but magazines have been building a strong online presence for some time. The *BusinessWeek* Web site (www.business-week.com) has led the way (for magazines) in providing updated business information and opinion quickly. As you can see in Figure 3.22, the site is busy, but segmented.

Figure 3.22   *The BusinessWeek Web site.*

When you scroll down the page, the left side of the site (below the menu bar) has the same features: the top story at the top followed by breaking news from the Associated Press, and then a quote from the featured blog of the day. In the Featured Blogs section, you can view many other *BusinessWeek* blogs or leave a comment about the quote.

BusinessWeek doesn't rely only on blogs. If you continue to scroll down the page, you'll see a section called BusinessWeek Extras, as shown in Figure 3.23. Here you can download podcasts, have people receive e-mail newsletters and alerts, set up the *BusinessWeek* Mobile site to receive *BusinessWeek* updates on your mobile phone, and more.

Figure 3.23   *The BusinessWeek Extras section.*

KCBS Radio, San Francisco

In 2009, KCBS, the first ever broadcasting radio station, celebrated its centennial. Obviously, the station has gone through quite a few changes since it was founded, and it has been an all-news station since 1968. For most of its history, KCBS and its predecessors were on the AM dial only (not available on the FM dial, not available on computer, not available on the Web, and not available on any social networking sites).

Over the past few years, KCBS has been working to build its online presence. As of this writing, KCBS can be listened to on computers through its online player accessible via its Web site at http://www.kcbs.com. At the top of the page are podcasts that you can download or subscribe to, as shown in Figure 3.24.

When you scroll down the page below all the news of the day, you'll see a pair of links to the KCBS Facebook and Twitter pages. When you subscribe to the Twitter feed, you'll get news updates (in case you prefer not to listen on your computer). When you open the KCBS Facebook page, you can link to the KCBS Web site (and its podcasts), as shown in Figure 3.25, and listeners can leave feedback.

Figure 3.24   *The KCBS Web site, with podcasts available for download.*

Figure 3.25   *The KCBS Facebook page.*

Summary

You have many different options when it comes to the types of blogs you can create and the blog platforms you can choose from. This chapter gave you an overview of several different types of popular blog platforms, and also discussed how to use different types of blog platforms. The case studies in this chapter could get your own creative juices flowing and provide inspiration about how to create blogs, what type of blogs to create, and how to integrate them with your other online offerings.

Before you do that, however, it's important to know how to blog responsibly, so let's continue on to Chapter 4.

4

Blogging Responsibly

In the online and offline worlds, people chat and share opinions about businesses, products, and services. Whether it is a word of mouth endorsement, written on a Facebook wall, or a quick chat with a colleague over lunch, chances are, the public is already discussing your company in some form or another.

By learning how to engage the talkers through open, online channels, you can truly connect with your customers. With a business blog, you not only get your messaging out to your audience, but you also bring your audience's comments in, making your blog the home base for these online conversations.

Listen to Your Audience

Listening to your audience and enabling it to speak builds a trust that can motivate your readers to help you spread the word. When your audience members are ambassadors for your blog (and as a result, your brand), the impact of what you write can extend far beyond your own existing reach. Audience members will carry a message about your blog or brand.

The following sections discuss the importance of "listening," covering topics such as two-way discussions, listening by sharing, tools to help you listen, and listening to what is being said.

Two-Way Discussions

Often, news blasts and company updates are one-way transmissions from a business to a recipient list or client base. With blogging, everything becomes more personal, creating more intimate and specialized discussions through content sharing. Opening up your blog to facilitate two-way discussion can help build and maintain your audience through acknowledgment of and encouragement of their input.

A comment form lets your readers know that you value their input, feedback, and commentary. These audiences of readers, clients, and potential customers want to be engaged in discussions and know that their opinions matter to your business.

According to Technorati's State of the Blogosphere 2008 (see Figure 4.1), when bloggers are online engaging in Web 2.0 activities, 84% comment on articles or blog posts. These bloggers also have commenting enabled on their blogs, which allows readers to add to what they have just read, make suggestions, or answer a question posed in the entry. Bloggers are social beings. Conversational bloggers, whether on their own blog or others, open entire sites to various audiences.

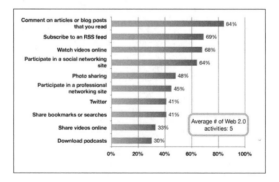

Figure 4.1 *Technorati's State of the Blogosphere 2008.*

A blog with a conversational tone, while still being professional, welcomes the audience to become a part of what you are creating and broadcasting. Through comments and feedback, you can get a feel for what makes your audience and customers tick, and you can tailor your posts to meet their needs. By requesting feedback, polling your audience, or asking a question at the end of your blog post, you put out the welcome mat for readers to add their two cents to the discussion you started. By responding to these comments, or even updating your post if they provided new information for your topic, it helps you engage in a blog-hosted conversation with your readers.

In the professional blogging realm, comments are highly regarded. When a reader feels moved enough by your content to write a message, you can use this to measure your blog's success. Comments show that your blog has achieved a valuable bidirectional communications platform.

The purpose of a business blog is to connect with existing or potential clients or customers, so it's important to make sure your blog achieves this open, two-way discussion. Without a two-way communications platform, readers aren't free to elaborate and share information, which is a key element to growing your site's visibility and audience. Two-way discussion lets readers know you are open to hearing their thoughts and opinions, and it lets them know your business values information sharing.

The information you share is not the final word. Instead, it should encourage comments and conversation from your readers. This "dialogue" creates a community feeling that makes readers comfortable with your online space.

Listening by Sharing

You can also reach your audience through listening by "sharing." The following subsections tell you how.

Getting Feedback Through Polls and Contests

One way to encourage discussion and feedback is through polls that enable readers to vote for their favorite options or picks.

In a web poll you can give your audience multiple choices or a chance to select their favorite options. Polls could be used for the blog itself, such as "Would you like to see more photos on this blog? Yes, No, Other (please leave a comment)". They can also be used to get product feedback; for example, "Do you like our company's new logo?" or "What color should the logo be?"

Since polls are limited to pre-set responses you'll often find even more feedback or expanded answers in the comments section of your post.

Contests are also a great crowd pleaser. When readers' opinions are considered with regard to a new ad campaign or perhaps a logo for a business, those readers feel a sense of ownership, knowing their opinions truly matter to the company. People love seeing something they've created being used online (when credited appropriately), so hosting a contest is a great way to show your readers that you appreciate their input while showcasing their talents.

For Super Bowl XLIII, Doritos sponsored a contest that solicited audience-submitted commercials that were then added to its Web site, crashthesuperbowl.com. Those ads then went through several rounds of voting before a winner was selected. The ad that ended up running during the Super Bowl, created by ad-making amateur readers of the Doritos site, was hailed by many as the best Super Bowl commercial of 2009. The ad was also the TiVO "stop watch" winner for the first half of the game, meaning more people went back on their TiVOs to view this ad than any other during the broadcast. Doritos was grateful to the two unemployed brothers from Batesville, Indiana, who created the popular commercial.

In 2009, for the upcoming Super Bowl XLIV, Doritos has been using the public video-sharing website Vimeo (http://www.vimeo.com/user2312887) to promote the contest using the previous year's winners in the videos. These videos can be embedded and shared on other blogs so that viewers can spread the message or enter the contest for 2010.

Using Images or Photos

To complement the text on your blog, you should also use images. Many bloggers use popular photo-sharing sites such as Flickr.com to showcase their images or host the photos they then add to their blogs. With Flickr.com, you can create public groups, through which readers can share photos with the group. Companies can create Flickr accounts and start groups (composed of their prospective audiences) to encourage photo sharing.

If your company sells blue jeans, you could set up the group so that anyone with photos of themselves or others in blue jeans can add their images. Your audience is then showcased in your group. Flickr group images can be made into slideshows that can be embedded into your blog. Suddenly your blog content is populated by readers' submitted images. You aren't simply putting your images and your message out but you're showcasing your audience.

You may also want to consider using submitted photos on your own blog (only with permission, of course). If you do so, remember to link to the original blogger's Web site. Doing so showcases their images and reminds them that you value how your customers use your products. Flickr.com also enables you create slideshows of images currently submitted to the group.

Consider the example of Libre Tea, makers of loof-leaf tea containers (http://libretea.com). Libre Tea's Flickr group allows anyone to share what they call "tea moments." They encourage you to take a photo when you are enjoying a cup of tea, whether on the go or at home. They then highlight these photos on their Web site. These pictures show how versatile the Libre Tea containers are, and they also inspire ideas about how to unwind and enjoy the product.

As you can understand from this example, two-way blogging discussions occur not only with text but with other forms of content, too. When you encourage readers to share their content with you (instead of just you sharing your information with them), you create a different level of interaction and engagement for the audience, making your blog a two-way street of information.

Tools to Help You Listen

On most platforms, when you open your site to comments, you can request a commenter's URL (for a blog or Web site, for example). This is another way to gauge your audience, such as whether they work in a similar business, write similar blogs, or do not have Web sites of their own. For example, if you discover your readers are predominantly other bloggers or more Internet-savvy, you can formulate specific ways to interact with them on your blog.

Publishers can use standard blog comment forms that come with their platforms or they can use tools to follow conversations about their site across the Web. The following subsections discuss various tools that enable you to listen to what people are saying about your blog.

Tracking Mentions

Google Alerts is the most basic way to find mentions of your site online. You can create custom alerts so that every time your brand, product, service, or company name is mentioned on the Internet, Google will send you an email alert. Figure 4.2 shows the Google Alerts Setup page.

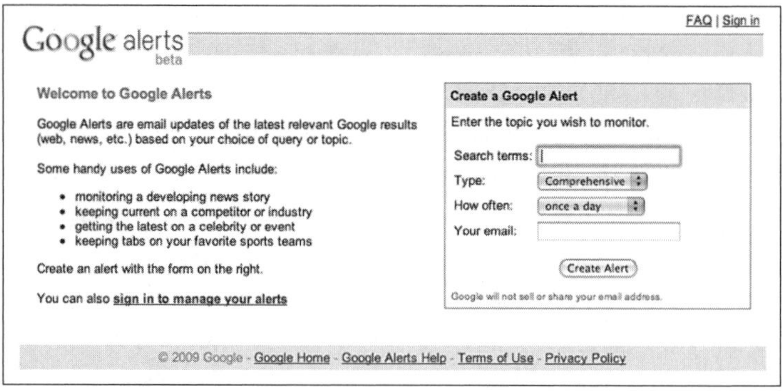

Figure 4.2 *Google Alerts Setup page.*

ChatCatcher (http://chatcatcher.com) is a service that enables blog publishers to find links from other blogs to their posts and any Twitter updates that include the link to the post. After they are installed, the services crawl the Internet to find mentions of your links; they add them at the bottom of your posts as regular comments, citing sources.

Visit http://search.twitter.com to search the Twitter service for instant mentions. The popular microblogging service is used by millions worldwide, and it enables 140-character updates that can include anything from links to favorite sites to comments about what the user had for lunch that afternoon. Twitter's brief character limit enables short conversations to lead to expanded discussions online and offline.

Because the Twitter service is fully searchable, you can use the search function to find any user in the world who is including any word in their updates at any time. All words posted in updates on Twitter are searchable and the Twitter search archive keeps this documented for several weeks.

Often, popular words and phrases are tracked using hash tags (pound signs). This hash tag feature comes in handy when you want to track specific events, such as a conference. For example, if you are an attendee at the 123 Conference, you can include #123Conference in a Twitter update and encourage other attendees to do the same. You can then track all #123Conference updates with ease using the http://search.twitter.com page and typing in the keywords in the search box. The search results will then display all mentions of #123Conference, from all Twitter users.

Twitter also lists its top 10 trending topics on the sidebar of all profile pages. These are words or hashtagged topics that have been posted in Twitter updates the most frequently.

Using this intuitive search feature, you can enter your search terms and find those on Twitter who are currently discussing a topic pertaining to your business.

When I was traveling and looking for a hotel, I wrote the following Twitter update: "Looking for hotel recommendations for San Francisco #WordCamp in the Union Square Area." Another Twitter user replied with the following: "@Miss604 Check out the Kimpton Hotels www.kimptonhotels.com". Within a few hours, Kimpton found the Twitter conversation and replied, "@Miss604 we hope you'll let us take care of u in SF. We have 9 hotels here. DM if you would like insider info on any." As you can guess, I ended up staying at a Kimpton hotel because of this attention to my conversation. The person running their Twitter account was searching Twitter for specific keywords, perhaps "hotels" or their company name "Kimpton," and my conversations appeared.

Site Statistics

The same type of tracking can be used to find mentions of your specific blog posts. By locating these links, you can get an idea of your reach and your audience. You can see who is listening, who is responding, and who thought your content valuable enough to expand upon or link in their own post. This also creates the opportunity for you to leave comments on other sites. You can thank the author for linking your site, or comment on the content they have written in their post. The simplest way to find incoming links is to use a statistics tracking program. These tools, mostly online, enable you to set up an account after which you can paste specifically generated code into your Web site so that it can begin tracking your statistics.

Google offers Google Analytics, which produces detailed statistical data after 23 hours, or you can use instant trackers such at SiteMeter (http://sitemeter.com) or StatCounter (http://statcounter.com). There are also platform-specific tracking systems available, such as Mint (http://haveamint.com) for WordPress users (see Figure 4.3).

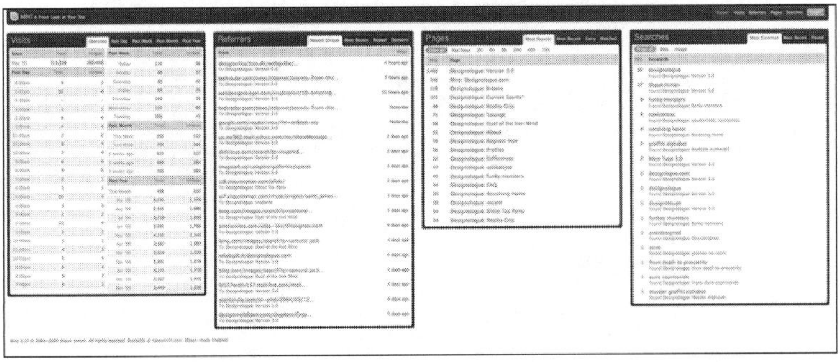

Figure 4.3 *Mint: Statistics for your Web site or blog.*

Most statistic-tracking systems show you who is coming to your site and their origin online, such as a link from another site or a search engine result. You can also see the readers' IP addresses, and which browser they are using to view your blog. By using these statistic-tracking applications on your site, you can see data such as the geographical location of your audience and what type of computer they are using to access your content.

Using this statistical data, you can determine whether your audience is using out-dated browsers (an understanding that will come in handy in terms of your blog's design specs), if they are on a Mac of PC, and if they are mostly mobile readers.

Your Mobile Audience

You want to make sure that your blog is viewable across any platform (browser or computer type).

The popularity of mobile devices is growing, so including tests to make sure your blog is compatible with these tools is beneficial. To test, simply access your blog from a mobile device and see if it displays the same way as when you look at it from a web browser on your computer. Sometimes blogs optimized for larger viewing might not be able to fit all information onto a tiny mobile screen. To help with this, you can use applications or services that will display your blog's post and/or pages in a way that is optimized for mobile viewing.

Some applications, such as Mobify.me (http://mobify.me) and plug-ins for blogging platforms such as WordPress, directly target mobile audiences.

WordPress users can download the WPtouch plug-in to convert their blog for reading in mobile devices (see Figure 4.4). After the plug-in has been activated on the blog, it requires a few tweaks to the settings before your site is ready to go mobile.

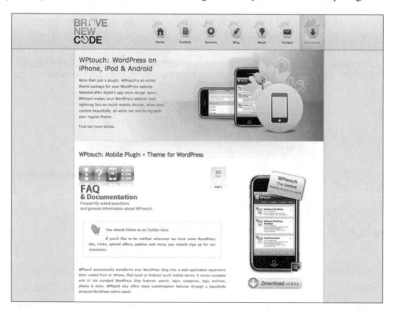

Figure 4.4 *WPtouch for WordPress by BraveNewCode.*

By knowing how your audience is accessing your content and by listening from behind the scenes to their viewing needs, you can optimize their reading experience on your site.

Listen to What's Being Said

Although your goal is not purely to encourage comments, it's definitely a factor in the success of your blog. You need to post something that readers find worth expanding on, or better yet, that they reference in their own blog posts.

When your work is referenced (with a link) in another's post, that reference is called a trackback. A trackback shows up as a comment; however it's simply a message notifying the author that someone has linked to their blog post. Your commenting system should be set up to allow trackbacks. After all, trackbacks notify you when someone has expanded on your thoughts or deemed them worthy of reference, and it enables the conversation you started to be expanded on in other blogs, ultimately expanding your reach. Others will see your openness to the conversation, and through mentions on blogs or sharing on social bookmarking sites, your work will be passed along organically.

People are talking about your company, its services, and its products, and you can't stop that. However, you can make yourself aware of these conversations. By using tools to track links and mentions, you can then engage in these outside discussions to record new feedback, clarify data, or just to show appreciation for the writer's interest in your business. Suppose, for instance, that you run an amusement park and find a blog post online about someone's experience on your roller coaster. That is a prime opportunity to show you are listening. If the roller coaster ride was a positive experience, you can leave a comment and thank them for their patronage, or perhaps encourage them to stop by again in the future. You could even link their post on your own blog, either in a blog post or on your blogroll or link list. In a blog post, you could showcase the positive experience the author had at your establishment and let others know that you truly value the patronage. Suddenly, a blog post becomes a fantastic marketing tool to highlight your business. Should the post have a negative tone, use your discretion to escalate the feedback to client services or drop a comment to let the author know you are looking into the matter (and be sure to follow up).

With negative feedback published online, your goal should not be to control the message by demanding the author remove the content (unless it is defamatory and in need of escalation). Your mission should be to embrace the feedback and handle it with care and tact. Letting authors know you are listening and that you value their opinion can go a long way in terms of a customer's impression of your company.

Comments and Responding to Them

Having a comments section on your site lets your readers know that their input is just as valued as the information you are presenting. However, you will receive several types of comments. You need to be prepared for whatever might be submitted.

Comment Forms

Most standard comment forms request the user's name, e-mail, and Web site for authentication, which is a good idea if you want to know about the person leaving the message. If your blogging platform contains these options, you can activate or deactivate them at any time. For an extra measure of protection against spam, you can request that commenters complete a captcha form (either an image or text) before their comment can be submitted. Captcha generators can be found online and pasted into your platform's settings. These scrambled images feature letters and numbers that need to be typed before the message can be sent. This level of authentication ensures that human beings and not spam-generating computer programs are leaving the comment messages. Captcha authentication might seem like overkill, but if you are having problems with spam comments, it's an option you should consider.

With all these fields in place, you can determine who is visiting your site and how best to reply to comments or follow up on an issue. When replying to comments in your own thread, it is courteous to direct your response to the message's original author. Some blog sites use the Twitter "@" reply method to target their replies (for example, "@John Smith, thank you for the feedback!"

When to Moderate Comments

Comments are an option on most blog platforms, and the commenting tool usually includes the option to moderate. Moderation is when a completed comment form does not get published automatically but sits in a queue awaiting your approval. Learning when and how to moderate enables you to maintain control of all content that is published to your blog. This section describes some of the types of comments you'll receive.

Levels of Moderation

There are various levels of moderation available on most blogging platforms. The first, and the simplest, is to allow all comments that are submitted to be published. The next would be to allow all comments from previously approved authors. So for example, if a reader has already left a comment before on your blog, you can automatically approve the rest of their comments going forward. The next few levels of moderation depend on the author's preference and the settings they would like to put in place.

Anonymous Comments

Anonymous comments can come from anywhere (for example, from someone who was unable to properly complete a form, a malicious spam attack, or simply someone who does not wish to be identified). Having required fields helps to prevent anonymous comments, but you can also set up your blog so that anonymous comments are held for moderation. This means you will need to approve them before they go public.

Spam

When it comes to spam, most blogging platforms have ways to prevent these comments from being published automatically (especially if you have moderation settings in place). These comments can include multiple links, or simply unpleasant content you don't to share with the public on your site, so it is recommended you monitor your comments to find these. Once you have identified comments such as these, you can moderate them (unapproved them for publishing) or delete them entirely.

Overloading sites with links to spam sites is one of the goals of spam marketers. Having more links on your site boosts the spam site's ranking, and you don't want your site to be a vessel for this type of behavior. When moderating comments, use your best judgment to determine whether the comments should be held for approval. Comments can be set up so that any new message is moderated or you can leave them open to be posted automatically (see Figure 4.5). Moderation settings vary based on the platform you're using, but common features include indicators such as IP address tracking, holding a comment if there are links in the body of the text, or giving approval if the author is a returning user.

If you receive a comment that is hateful or simply not publishable because of questionable content, you can use your statistics-tracking program to log the IP address of the user. An IP address is a unique location marker for the user's access point to the Internet. You can then flag this IP address or set up features to automatically hold future comments from this user in the moderation queue. When a comment thread ceases to set a professional and respectful tone, negative messages can be deleted or held in moderation.

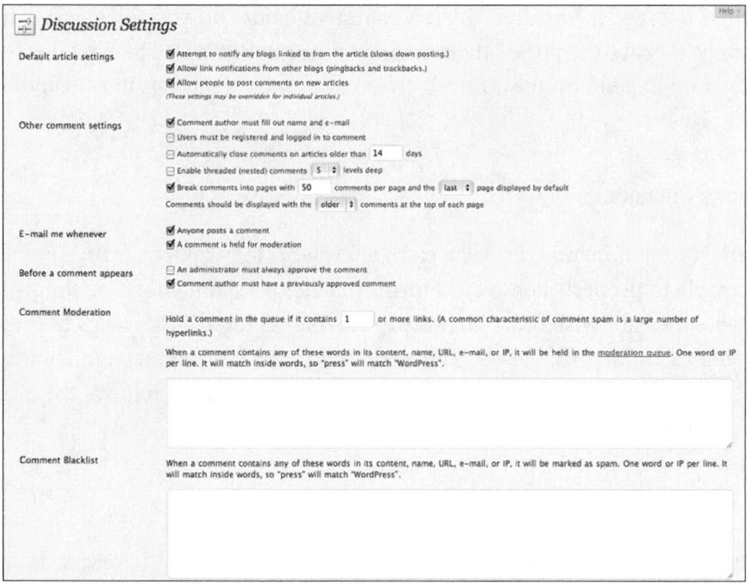

Figure 4.5 *Comment moderation on WordPress (WordPress.org).*

In some circumstances, you can contact the author if he has left an e-mail address. In this contact, you can let him know why you have held his comment (for example, foul language or defamatory content). Doing so lets the author know you are paying attention, and it enables the author to write something more concise and tactful. Commenters might not enjoy seeing their comment being held for moderation; however, this is a way to maintain control of the content on your site while still being approachable and reasonable.

Negative Feedback Can Help You Grow

If you receive a comment on a blog post that is less than complimentary, the manner in which you respond to the post reflects on your company. Participating in a flame war, or back-and-forth battles with an aggravated commenter, is not the most productive way to address an issue. Negative comments might not necessarily need to be deleted unless they are defamatory, libelous, or anything similarly malicious. However, if comments contain negative but productive feedback, you should respond in a courteous manner.

For example, suppose you are a clothing distributor and you have just published a blog post about a new pair of pants. A complaint is then received in the comments section from a customer who says she recently bought a pair and they already have a tear in them. You can approve the comment and reply directly, saying that it's unfortunate and you will be happy to have customer service follow up. You can then send the commenter's information to your customer service department; you'll have the customer's name and e-mail from the comment form. You can also link to the appropriate section of your site where customer concerns can be submitted. By dealing with this matter publicly, your audience will know you are attentive and you truly care about your customers.

Dealing with Negative Feedback

The saying "no news is good news" applies to the blogging world, too. When posts are positive and your readers are pleased and informed, they may not always leave a comment. However, when readers write something congratulatory, be sure to respond promptly and thank them for their participation on the blog.

A large part of blogging for your business is being personal and approachable (for your customers and readers) in your posts and within your comments section. Responses should be professional and respectful. (And so, grammar, punctuation, and common conversational courtesy should be adhered to.) You want to be informative and transparent and never immature in your replies, even if the original comment has set that tone.

Dealing with negative comments is a bit trickier, however, so here are some tips:

- Address negative comments on your own site as soon as possible so that they do not fester in the mind of the author and cause any adverse effects if they do not receive some type of response.

- If the comment is negative yet constructive or is conducive to a productive discussion, by all means feel free to approve it. Publishing negative feedback, and the way a company deals with it, can truly reflect on your brand in a positive way. Your readers come to your site for information and valuable content.

- Should the comment be destructive and critical of the blog post itself, your options are to hold it for moderation, delete it, or to take things offline.

- When a comment is libelous, allowing it to be published and responding publicly is not the best course of action. You can e-mail the commenter privately about sincere concerns (if they provided a valid e-mail address). Although the subject of being responsible for allowing libelous comments made by others to be published on your blog is technically a legal "gray area," it may still be deemed as slander. In severe cases, threats may need to be dealt with on a private/personal level. In most instances, however, the Delete key is all you need.

It is also important to protect other members of the community. Therefore, you should also monitor the discussions in your comments section for attacks between commenters.

In October of 2009, a ruling was made to settle a lawsuit between a group of plaintiffs and 30 people who posted anonymous and derogatory comments about them on an online message board called AutoAdmit. "According to the plaintiffs, the suit was necessary because the discussion board, a site designed for law school graduates, was often monitored by firms looking to hire. Because the comments were associated with their names, the women claimed that it would hurt their chances of being offered a job" (source: ReadWriteWeb http://www.readwriteweb.com/archives/watch_out_trolls_your_menacing_comments_could_lead_to_fines.php).

Case Study: Molson Coors Brewing Company

Molson Coors Brewing Company has been brewing since 1786 and produces some of North America's most popular brands of beer, including Molson Canadian, Coors Light, Molson Export, Molson Dry, and Rickard's. They are also partnered with worldwide labels such as Heineken, Corona, Miller Genuine Draft, Foster's Lager, and Tiger.

After Molson's merger with Coors in 2005, the company went from being purely Canadian to 50% U.S. owned, with headquarters in Montreal and in Denver, Colorado. Being Canada's oldest brewery and using the slogan "I am Canadian," suddenly Molson Canadian stopped looking so patriotic in the eyes of the consumers who felt a sense of national pride beaming from each maple-leaf-boasting bottle.

With this new identity crisis, the public and media struggled with their perception of the brand. Molson's chief public affairs officer, Ferg Devins, said that this became the best time to start telling their company's story. In 2007, they launched the "Molson in the Community" blog and began covering all aspects relating to the business, the industry, their 3,000 employees, partnerships, and consumers online (see Figure 4.6).

Hosting a blog for a beer company does have its challenges and requires effort in moderating comments and content in a tactful manner. Devins explains the types of comments the company holds for moderation given the nature of the industry: "We need to make sure that there's no one talking about excessive consumption or under-legal drinking age consumption."

Figure 4.6   *The Molson Coors in the Community blog.*

The blog created by Molson made the company approachable to many online, which caused a few problems in terms of customer feedback. They were seeing a trend where consumers were leaving comments when they had a general company inquiry. In these cases, Molson was able to funnel these messages to the appropriate department in the company.

Tonia Hammer, Molson's community relations coordinator, uses Google Alerts along with Truecast and Radian6 to scan the Internet for mentions of their products or brands. Using these tools to monitor incoming links and mentions online, the company came across some backlash online regarding its nationwide blogger outreach campaign, Brew 2.0.

Brew 2.0 was an event held in various cities across the nation where bloggers were invited to a Molson brewery for an evening of beer education. The event received high praise from participants and throughout the online media sphere. The company's intentions, however, were questioned on several blogs, which truly put Molson's social media practices to the test. Having set up alerts so that they can be notified of mentions online, Molson was able to find the discussions and chime in, officially. In particular, one blogger questioned not only the process Molson used to create their invite list for the Brews 2.0 events, but also their commercial motives.

"What it really came down to in the end was the particular people that were criticizing what we had done [with Brew 2.0]," says Devins. "They had this position that we reached out to the wrong people and that it was too strategic."

Adam Moffat, manager, marketing and brand public relations, explains how Molson addressed these concerns in the blogosphere. "We don't want to get pulled into an argument—there's no hope of changing [the author's] opinion; we just wanted to provide clarity on information that they misunderstood, being transparent about what our goal was for this activity." Devins adds that public responses should always be deferential. "If it's opinion, we'll counter with our opinion, but we'll also be respectful to people being entitled to their opinion." However, when it comes down to the straight facts about their company, "if someone's got information that they're transmitting wrongfully, or they're not on the mark, or it's not fact-based—we will definitely come in hard with facts," says Devins.

In this case, Moffat noted that one of the most gratifying parts of being transparent and addressing these concerns online is that Brew 2.0 participants can find these discussions and are able to band together, defending the company simply because they believe in the goals of their online community.

Molson believes that the successful Brew 2.0 event helped them bridge a gap between consumer and company and connected online entities. Devins describes it as going beyond blogging and "into a broader scope of business."

The Molson in the Community blog has also become a tool for employee engagement, and as Devins notes, "It's reaching out to our people at the field level. From the ground up, not from the corner suite."

Blog posts nurture the pride and engagement of the employees, sharing what they do in the field and building the corporate community though this online platform. "Employees across the country are able to tell their story and what they're doing in the community through the blog," said Moffatt. With this outlet, "We're just really doing a better job of publicizing the great work that's being done within our walls, but also out in the community by our employees."

Sample blog posts include "Eric Molson Retires After 50 Years at Canada's Brewery," "The Beer Store Bottle Drive For Leukemia May 23–24," "Calgary Sales Team Plays Their Part at Calgary Inter-Faith Food Bank." They even offer up their blog to guest posts, such as the entry, "A Post by Marcy Robertson, YMCA Relationship Development Manager."

Since hosting Brew 2.0, Molson has become involved with the global Twestival event (which raised $250,000 through Twitter in more than 200 cities), and have signed on to be a part of a social media strategy for the Vancouver 2010 Olympics.

Sharing stories online with the blog goes beyond the walls of the company. "[The blog] has given us more breadth and depth with respect to our philanthropic effort because we're able to tell and share a story," says Devins. "It's humanizing our company and it's humanizing our brand," adds Moffatt.

"No longer do consumers want that faceless monolith preaching at them," says Moffat. They want to feel closer to brands and companies, and certainly given that our company is a social one in its roots and DNA, it certainly just makes a lot of sense that we act in this way."

Summary

Now that you know some best practices, you need to determine your own moderation levels through instant feedback. However, before you can get audience reactions, you need to serve up that great content, worth commenting upon. For inspiration, in the next chapter you'll see some innovative writing concepts from companies across many different industries.

5

Finding Topics to Write About

After you have decided to start a blog, you must next find something to write about on a regular basis. When you're passionate about a topic, it should be easy enough to find subject matter. However, one is always in need of inspiration, especially when it comes to publishing fresh content. Blog posts can include news, insights, information, photos, lists, polls, questions, and almost any other form of content. Finding the content and subject matter that works best for your company can help you establish a strong publishing pace and keep your readers engaged. Being passionate about your subject matter adds value for the reader of your blog and keeps you interested in its maintenance. As your company is certainly already passionate about its products and industry, your blog will let that shine through.

Writing Blogs for the Wider World

When creating content on a public blog, the goal is to attract readers and appeal to a wider audience. By making your content interesting and then searchable, readers not only find your blog but they will stick around to see what else you have to share. The following sections explore how to write your blog to gain exposure and a wider audience.

Creating an Industry Resource Blog

Blog topics can cover everything from your own company news to industry updates and information. By supplying a wide scope of reading material and multimedia, your blog can become a one-stop shop for those seeking news and updates for content that pertains to your entire industry. Readers shouldn't need to go anywhere else if they've subscribed to your feed that is complete with a wide range of topics.

An example of an industry resource blog is a winery with a blog that updates its readers about varietals, seasonal offerings, and wine-making processes. By peppering in posts that include tips on wine making, maintaining vineyards, growing grapes, and profiling wine regions, the site becomes much more than a wine blog. Readership expands to those seeking material about wine in general, which you provide, and in turn, readers discover your business and product offerings. This concept can be applied to any business or industry.

By providing industrywide information, and not just specifics about your own company, you can gain an audience perfectly tailored to your business. With your blog being an online hub, it connects you with current and potential customers by being a true all-in-one resource for your field.

This also shows that your company is in touch with its industry and is keeping up with the latest news and trends. It fits in with the concept of opening up the floor for discussion with your customers and potential clients while catering to their need for information.

Blogging about the world outside your company (but still within your industry) can turn one-time readers into subscribers. Audiences are repeatedly drawn to blogs if they know they can get regular updates that are not only about a favorite company, but paired with practical tips and industry insights each time they visit.

This is not to say you need to spend exorbitant amounts of time and effort writing in-depth articles about the past, present, and future of your market. However, by providing useful information, data, facts, and links to other articles, you can help build your profile and presence online.

Whole Foods Markets, a leader in the natural and organic foods industry, operates several online and social network presences and maintains a blog, called The Whole Story. The blog features in-store events, offerings from the company such as recipes and coupon books, and highlights of partner growers. The blog also talks about food in general (see Figure 5.1).

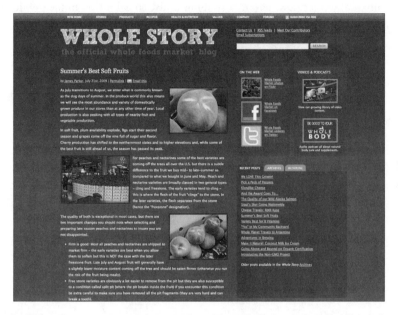

Figure 5.1   *"Summer's Best Soft Fruits" from The Whole Story, the official Whole Foods Market blog.*

You can essentially go to any grocery store or market to purchase your ripe summer fruit; however, with an informative blog to remind you of seasonal treats, how to make your selection, and highlights of varieties, you may be more likely to visit the local Whole Foods. Nowhere in the blog post does it mention that Whole Foods has the best fruit. Instead, it simply features the product (which is available at Whole Foods Market). Readers may conclude that if a market knows so much about fruit and other foods (enough to write about it and inform the world online), it would be worth a trip to one of its stores to check out these offerings.

By branching out and covering all things pertaining to your industry, your blog can bridge any physical distance between you and your customers and even answer questions before they're asked. For example, if you're in the clothing business and your customer service department receives several calls about how to water-treat the jackets you sell, you could write a blog post about the process. In a written post or even a video, you can provide tools and tips for product care. By doing this, you provide interesting content for readers and an added value service.

Public relations firm Hill & Knowlton operates a group blog with contributions from several staff members (see Figure 5.2). They also aggregate or republish content from other blogs that they find informative. Their spin on having a company blog introduces their client base to new elements of public relations. Each author from the company is given a biography page, and their content includes information, links, and interviews about how about to use social media in the public relations industry.

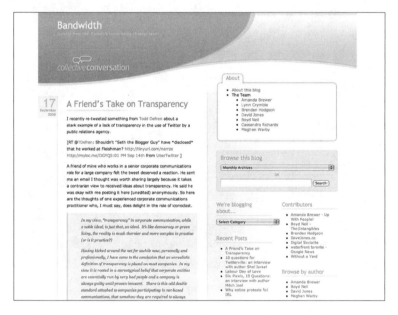

Figure 5.2   *Hill & Knowlton's Collective Conversation Bandwidth blog.*

Helpful and useful information you share in blog posts provides content for a specific audience of customers and clients and an entire world of potential connections who might just stumble across your post online. By having this content on your blog, it will come up in Internet search results. Perhaps someone will search for "water treating jackets." Chances are, they may just stumble across the blog post you published. By writing the post, using the proper keywords, and providing this extra content for your readers, a whole new audience may discover your business through searches.

Create an Online Community

Although a blog is a part of your company's home on the Internet, the best way to grow your audience is to give your audience a sense of ownership of the space. You do this by being open to discussions and hosting interactive content on your blog to create a strong online community.

In some cases, Internet users will create groups, fan pages, or their own blogs dedicated to various products or services they like. Opening up similar access and playgrounds for discussion in your own online space can work to your advantage. By having a community of readers, supporters, and individuals who share your links and content, you can amplify your message. The community might not necessarily be an actual page, forum, or comments section but you'll find that your readers will become your blog (and your company's) evangelists. Through that connection, they create a sense of community.

You can help nurture this community by having a blog that promotes conversation with comments, where the author is also engaged. You also need to share what you've posted by allowing readers to copy and paste your latest link to their social networking accounts, by bookmarking it, or by e-mailing it to their colleagues. If your blog generates its own community, it can also reach out to online spaces or social networks where other communities lie.

To branch out and encourage this cross-pollination of content, you can arm your community with the following blog-sharing tools:

- Have the tools available. Provide links and "submit this" or "share this" buttons on your blog posts (see the AddThis service in Figure 5.3). Encourage readers to pass along your link through social bookmarking sites such as Digg, Delicious, Reddit, Newsvine, and Facebook.

- Twitter also has several plug-ins and widgets (such as Tweetmeme) that cut long blog post URLs into easy-to-share links that are short enough for the service's 140-character limit.

- Readers can also share content through their own blogs, should they also be online content producers. There are no other steps to provide should they want to link back to your post. However, be on the lookout for the trackback so that their link is visible from your site.

Providing your readers with these online sharing tools so that they can help spread your brand for you is a great way to expand your reach and draw others into your online community.

As evangelists for your blog, through sharing and promoting your content, your readers also become ambassadors of your brand. Arming these loyal followers can involve anything from providing the online space in which they can hold discussions (such as comment forms) to supplying promotional items (perhaps offering them a discount code). Your blog in some ways act like a loyalty program, rewarding readers and the audience for stopping by through a coupon code or contest giveaways.

Figure 5.3 *AddThis bookmarking and sharing service for blogs.*

You can also give your brand ambassadors tools such as logo badges for their own site so they can indicate that they read or are a fan of your blog. You could also make your content easily shareable (for example, by posting your videos to YouTube or by using the previously mentioned bookmarking tools).

With your blog as the home base of conversations and content for your company, people can find the most accurate information they seek right from the source. As your links and posts are shared, you will draw a bigger and expanded audience to your community. And even though you might not have a profile on other networks where your links, posts, or images are being shared, if a reader submits your story to these services, the audiences there will be drawn back to your site to read the article.

According to a 2009 report by the social bookmarking website AddToAny.com, Facebook has replaced e-mail as the number one way people share links to content online. According to the poll, 24% of the time someone passed along a link, it was through Facebook, while 11% of the time it was by e-mail, and Twitter link sharing accounted for 10.8%.

Case Study: Canucks Fan Zone

It's hard to find a professional sports team that doesn't already have an audience or a large fan base, but it is a challenge to make that audience feel connected. In the fall of 2007, Jamie Ollivier and Bruce Warren of Anton Sledgehammer Creative were brought in by the Vancouver Canucks National Hockey League team to boost its community, both on and offline.

With the Canucks, it was a matter of connecting the 18,000 people in the stands at games with those at home, in pubs, and across the world who wanted to support the team in any way they could. Working together with the organization, they came up with the Canucks Fan Zone, the first of its kind in the NHL. It engages fans online by hosting forums, allowing for user-generated content, blog posts, and linking out to other Canucks bloggers and podcasters. According to Warren, Anton Sledgehammer Creative wanted to make sure there was an arena to allow the fans to cover the team and get the recognition they deserved as loyal Canucks followers.

The Fan Zone is different from the main site, Canucks.com. As Ollivier explains, "One is where people can express themselves, and the other is where people get paid to write." The Fan Zone has an entire page dedicated to linking to other Canucks blogs and podcasts while welcoming commentary and feedback from what Warren calls the "nonwriting" fans. The goal is to extend the online audience from the bloggers themselves (who often follow other bloggers) to those who would just want to consume and appreciate the content that is published.

The duo understood from the start that things would still need to be authentic and transparent by fans and for the fans. "We understand that if things are not organic, people will reject them," said Ollivier. "We're a bit like gardeners. We look at what's working and what things are catching on, and then we can feed and water those things. Because you have a million plants going, only a few are really going to hit… whatever's going to be the most effective is what we're going to be pouring our efforts into."

The efforts paid off as fans from New Zealand, China, and across the globe now had a place online to gather all their Canucks information and to share how they feel about the team. As a result of their online engagement, in the spring of 2009 the Canucks had as many Facebook fans (in its group and page) as the entire NHL. The Fan Zone also bumped up Canucks.com to being the number one team site in the league. The difference made by the Fan Zone was noticeable as Warren compared the statistics chart (fittingly) to a hockey stick.

Anton Sledgehammer Creative could not have achieved all of this without the forward-thinking nature of those in the Canucks organization such as president and CEO, Chris Zimmerman, who they say really understood the potential of the entire campaign.

"The thing about the Fan Zone is that it allows the Canucks to acknowledge that the fans are really important and that the fans are what power the team. Without them, the team is nothing," said Ollivier. "By empowering the fans, you're basically filling up your gas tank."

Ollivier also noted that the Fan Zone gives a new venue in which fans can express themselves other than cheering. "That's really been the big difference because then people feel like they're a part of something because they have been acknowledged by the brand that they are a part of something—a part of the tribe."

The Fan Zone concept not only engages bloggers and contributors but also opens up the entire platform for regular fans who would like to watch, connect, or share their own thoughts. With the success they've seen in the 2009 season, it's a concept that is now being duplicated and replicated across the league.

Creating an Internal Blog (or Blogs) for Your Company

The ease of publishing content to a blog makes it an attractive platform for information sharing, whether in the public realm or privately on a closed intranet within a company. Users can add content, share links, and provide updates even if they are not shared with the public. Having this outlet can improve communications within a company and perhaps raise morale by promoting a job well done.

There are several ways that an internal or inward-facing company blog can benefit your company including boosting communications, getting feedback, and helping promote the great work the employees carry out each day.

Keep People Informed

Blogs are public platforms that are highly visible and searchable. However, they can also serve an internal, private purpose. In the same way that business blogs can help share and build a community between the company and its customers, a company blog can also bridge gaps within the organization.

Keeping your employees up-to-date on projects and events helps to promote a healthy team environment. Currently, the standard communication tool for companies is e-mail, along with internal memos, or perhaps proprietary messaging systems. By taking the information that might go into a mass e-mail and publishing it for the group in a closed online system, the data is more searchable while still reaching its intended audience.

Allowing employees to showcase their accomplishments, triumphs, and milestones with their peers is also a great morale booster. Promotions in companies are certainly something worth blogging and sharing with other team members. If a salesperson has a client success story to share or receives a recommendation or client testimonial, the blog is a great way to profile these achievements.

You can also use the blog to profile departments by posting company photos and biographies of new hires or long-standing employees. With large corporations, some departments rarely interact. This could leave you wondering what role the dozen other people in the lunchroom with you play in their daily life with the company. Having an internal blog can put names to faces more effectively than the annual company picnic.

Communications from all branches can include the following:

- Notes from HR about company policies or social events such as birthdays

- A message from the CEO about company changes, updates, or even a holiday greeting

- A posting from administration about things happening in the company's building, such as a monthly fire drill

- Updates on projects to keep everyone in the loop

- Hosting contests for employees or an online poll such as, "name the new product" or "help us choose the new logo"

Departments can also be featured with photo galleries and biographies, should that information be free to share. Those involved with specific projects can also use the blog to not only post updates but to also ask questions of their team. The comments section can be used to brainstorm and provide feedback, while the blog post publishing platform can share text, images, and links that may prove useful to the team.

Internal Blogs for Project Management

As with a regular business blog, an internal site must still remain professional and have the main goal of building your business, only from the inside out. It won't replace water-cooler chat, but it can give employees a safe, comfortable, team-oriented environment online where they can keep themselves current on the inner workings of their nine-to-five.

Be sure to create a set of guidelines for the blog (for example, what is acceptable content to share and rules for commenting). Assign a team member to moderate the blog, looking for comments, content to update, and making sure the site runs smoothly for all. You will also want the IT department on your side to ensure the internal site is not accessible from outside the company, especially if content pertains to sensitive or private product information.

An internal company blog is not a chat room and should not impede anyone's daily workflow. It is simply a resource on which professional information is shared within a department or companywide.

This blog could also help others collaborate on projects. For example, an image (design spec, potential logo, and so forth) could be shared, and employees could comment and leave constructive feedback. This would be quicker than e-mailing the image around, and all feedback would be in the same place (in the blog comments). The blog should be open to include all departments, and after it has been set up, communications should be sent around as an introduction and encourage others to participate. For example, if marketing begins an internal blog, this should be communicated to other departments and other teams should feel welcome to contribute as well.

Internally, a project blog helps track updates, tasks, and progress of a team effort. Various members can post content, comment, and provide input instantly. Issues can be tracked and searched, and the entire project can be documented in a simple, easy-to-read format that enables for multimedia.

Multimedia that can be published on blog posts includes photos and videos, and most video-sharing services offer an embedding code. This piece of text can be copied and pasted into a blog post to display a video player. If the video is not to be shared publicly, teams can upload video files through the blogging platform. The subject of these videos could be demonstrations, interviews, or product-related promotional content.

Internal blogs provide communication solutions for developers, sales teams, management, and all other employees of a company. Even though the platform itself is meant to be public and searchable, these same features can benefit your company in terms of productivity.

Departments can publish and track updates on projects and even employee news and announcements. Sharing information in real time and providing updates enables an entire workgroup or company to increase productivity through communication. Feedback can be provided in a secure environment that all can see, without flooding e-mail inboxes, and your company can have fully chronicled project notes.

Internal blogs with multiple authors (perhaps one from each department, with a central moderator) can keep everyone informed, promote projects, feature work, and showcase your valued employees.

Product Blog (External)

Having either an internal or external blog for a specific project or product enables you to showcase exciting developments, partnerships, and announcements with the world. Publicly, if privacy issues allow, you can essentially go from documenting the development stage of a product to building buzz about its progress and announcing its launch for your audience on your blog.

This is also a great way to reach your audience and use your blog for market research. Depending on the level of engagement you'd like to see from your audience for the project, you can create polls, ask for input, or even run contests to name the items or select features. The Eastman Kodak Company provides an online photo-sharing and photo-editing service through Ofoto.com. The Ofoto website has a blog (http://ofoto.typepad.com/) that keeps users informed about service updates and enhanced features (see Figure 5.4).

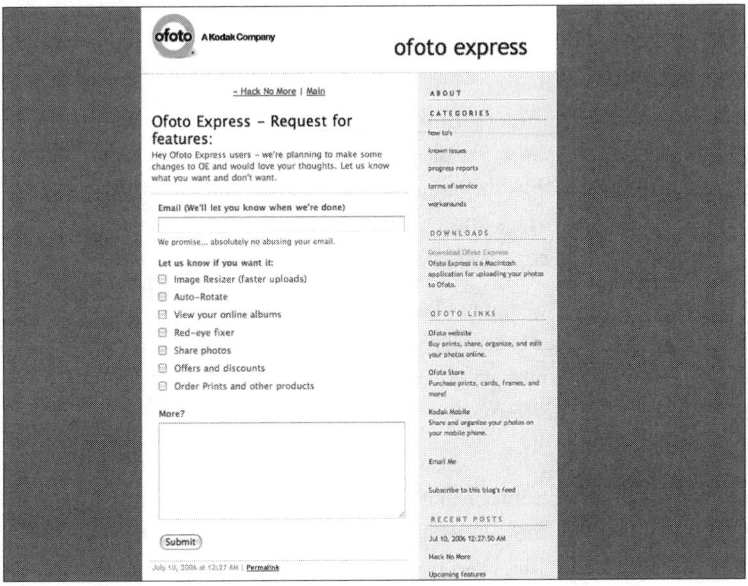

Figure 5.4 *The Eastman Kodak Company's Ofoto blog.*

Blog posts for Ofoto include updates, known issues, and upgrade announcements. Users can leave comments to provide feedback, say if the information was useful, or to suggest new features they would like to see provided with the service.

Because the service is public, it's only natural that they keep the public informed of upgrade and updates. They also welcome suggestions and respond to feedback in the comments section of the blog.

If committing to following and tracking the specific project or product on your blog, be sure to keep the content fresh by updating when there are new discoveries, updates, or changes. Be dedicated to following the entire life cycle.

Public project blogs should also not go dormant after a project is complete. You'll often see campaigns that use campaign-specific slogans as domain names. After the specific promotion has run its course, however, readers and customers do not have a reason to return to that site. To avoid this instant burnout, you can use your blogging platform's tags or category systems to classify all posts pertaining to the project (instead of creating a distinct domain).

When publishing a blog post, you can provide the author several options. You enter a title, content for the post, perhaps add an image, and also select tags or categories. By using these classification systems, the blog platform sorts your content, which makes it easy for readers to search archives and helps it get picked up in search engine results. Tags and categories are created by the author and saved so that later the author can simply check the box next to an existing tag and add the post to that classification.

For example, a blog post about a new vehicle could be tagged using the words *convertible, roadsters, performance*. In the future, whenever another post is written about this vehicle or a similar vehicle, the tags and categories can be checked so that the post is classified within the same searchable directory. Most blog platforms also create specific URLs for tags and categories. This way you can go to http://your-companyblog.com/tag/convertible to see all posts tagged as "convertible."

Tags and categories are a way of classifying your blog posts. Each tag and category receives its own link (for example, http://yourblog/category/umbrellas). Thus, readers can follow posts about a product that interest them, and they can also see all archived content for this item.

Tags and categories can also be assigned their own RSS feeds so that readers can subscribe to all of your content that is specifically tagged with a topic they want to follow. RSS, or Really Simple Syndication, is a way of subscribing to a blog or specific post categories. Readers can obtain this special link by clicking an RSS icon or "subscribe" link. Readers can then input this link into a feed reader, such as Google Reader, through which they can be instantly notified of news on the blogs they are following. The idea is that updates come to your feed reader inbox like unread e-mails so that you don't have to go out to each site and check whether there is new content.

Summary

In blogging, content is king. You can have great search terms that draw people in from search engines, but the key is to have content that keeps the reader captivated and motivated to return to your site or subscribe. The way in which you present your content helps engage your audience and encourage them to participate or become a part of your project. In this regard, blogs can be used internally for company use or they can be public-facing to promote and get exposure for your products, projects, and content.

With so many options for blog content and with so many individuals or departments potentially involved, it then becomes a question of who will write the content. The next chapter provides options for and examples of author contributions.

6

Who Will Write the Blog?

A business blog requires passion and dedication. After all, you must produce quality content on a regular basis. In companies of any size, finding someone to manage this can sometimes prove difficult. Some companies assign responsibility for the blog to an existing employee or department, making it everyone's responsibility but moderated by a single individual. Other companies hire someone to specifically handle their social media strategy and profiles.

Writing from Within a Company

A common question asked when companies consider starting a blog for their business is this: Who will author it? Companies have several options for this, but the optimal scenario under any option is to find someone willing to take on authoring responsibility. You need dynamic content that can be updated often, so finding room in existing job descriptions might not be easy.

When looking for a contributing writer, remember that someone who is passionate about a subject will provide the best content about that subject. (And readers can pick up on an author's passion and willingness to share on a blog.) Topics flow smoothly, discussions are created, and the author's enthusiasm for the subject matter becomes contagious.

The job of writing for a blog can be added to the author's job description. That description can note how many posts are required each week and any moderation duties. However, running a blog consists of much more than composing posts. You need to decide whether your author will take on the rest of the responsibilities that come with overseeing a blog. These responsibilities include coming up with content ideas, moderating comments, tracking statistics and metrics, setting up alerts online to monitor feedback, and so on. The author you use might not be the best fit for this entire scope of work. Therefore, having a separate person in charge of your social media plan might be necessary.

If you assign these management tasks to someone else, your authors can then focus on content. You may even want to create a Director of Social Media position so that one team member can manage social media elements and possibly gather material from multiple authors while monitoring the success and reach of the blog. Without a position such as this, management of the blog could inhibit the author's creative output, or might put too much on the author's plate if she is an existing employee who has expanded her job description. An entire department can also manage various tasks pertaining to the blog or take turns writing posts from different points of view.

Identifying Authors

An important step when starting out with a blog is to introduce the audience to the author. This can be done in the first blog post, on a page called "About" or in the sidebar of the blog.

Putting a name to a passage and having a subsequent biography page for that name allows readers to see where exactly the information is coming from within the company. This provides context and a more personalized look at the content that is presented.

Blog posts should convey the voice of their author, who should have a specific user-name assigned. When you sign up for a blogging service, Admin is the default user-name. However, you can assign your own chosen username to a blog account. After setting up the blog, just change Admin to a writer's name. Doing so not only adds security (because Admin is the most common username on blogs), but it also adds a level of personalization. Nothing makes a blog post seem more insincere than when it is signed Admin (and not by a "real" person in the company).

After you have your main administrator account set up, add more authors or begin blogging under the personalized author profile. Figure 6.1 shows more authors being added with WordPress.

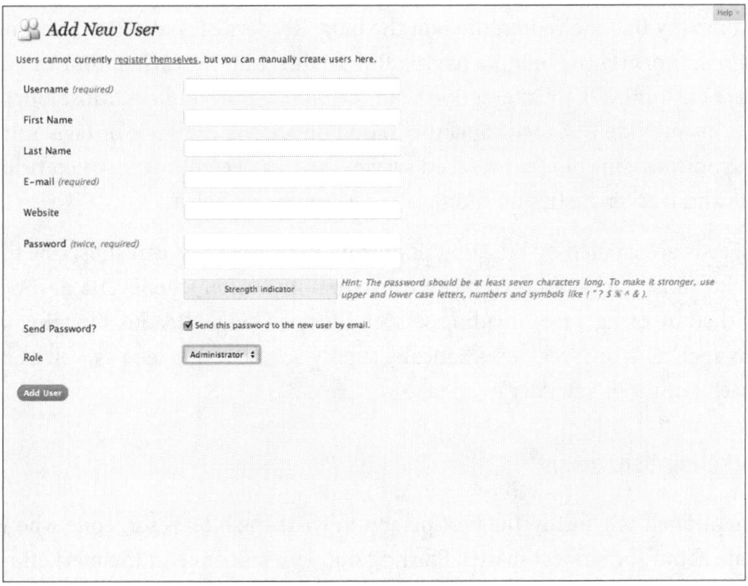

Figure 6.1 *Adding a new user on WordPress.org.*

Your blog's About page (or Biography page) should contain the names of the con-tributors and a few lines about their involvement with the company. This can include their name, title, location (if the company has multiple offices), and some-times a personalized icon called an avatar. This avatar can be set up to appear next to blog posts that are written by the blog's authors, helping the reader easily identify the writer of the post.

Multiple Authors

Having multiple authors is a great way to give depth to your blog's content while also saving some time with more than one contributor. By assigning multiple authors, you not only give many voices to the blog, but you get a more personal delivery of the specific content the specialized authors supply.

If more than one person from a department contributes to the blog, be sure to have appropriate author names and profiles in place for each. You do want to let your readers know who is "speaking" to them. In addition, crediting authors may lend credibility to blog posts, too. For example, a blog post by the CEO of the company will carry more weight than one written by an intern. In the same vein, a blog post written by "Bob in I.T." about a system status update will also be more applicable and personalized to the reader than a system status update from "Tina in Sales."

If you have multiple contributors, you can profile the entire team on the site. Doing so may draw attention to the diversity of the content and the multiple voices from the company that are represented on the blog. Readers may also become fans of certain authors on the blog, so having RSS feeds set up for each author can help readers customize their interaction with the blog and its authors. Most blogging platforms provide RSS feed capability based on author, category, or tags. You can also syndicate your blog or use feed services such as FeedBurner, which helps you create and track statistics on multiple feeds for your Web site.

RSS Feeds are created by blogging platforms so that readers can subscribe to the content. Subscribers can then receive instant notification whenever a new post is published by using a feed-reading service such as Google Reader. Blogging platforms such as WordPress automatically supply an entire site feed as well as a feed for each author or category.

The Marketing Department

As mentioned previously, the best person to write the blog is someone who is passionate about the subject matter. Starting out with someone in the marketing department would be a good fit. Marketing and communications professionals know how to address clients (and potential customers) while keeping the best interest of the company in mind, so this department is a good choice for managing the blog. In addition, blog writing should be consistent, personable, thought provoking, and interesting to the reader.

Composing a blog post isn't entirely different from preparing a press release. The biggest difference is in the messaging and the personality of the writing. For example, to complement a press release about a new product launch, you might hear the thoughts of "Jennifer from Marketing" on the matter. Her thoughts about this latest release or its specific campaign can be expressed in the blog, perhaps using her enthusiasm to pass along the company's excitement to the consumer.

Key elements of a press release include the headline; the subject line; the release body; the who, what, when, where, and why; company information; and contact information. Releases are tailored for news agencies to get picked up and are to the point in the hopes that larger stories will grow from its resources. Blog posts should also have keyword-rich headlines. However, the content should be used to inform and generate a discussion. Blog messaging can work in tandem with news releases to capture the attention of the online audience, while the release heads out to the rest of the world through various dissemination channels. Blog posts are usually immediate, but several blog publishing platforms also enable you to configure them for publication at a future date (much like embargoed press releases). They can also be edited at any time, which makes them more flexible than press releases. For example, if there is a typo on the release or perhaps the wrong contact information was given, the company will need to contact the newswire and issue a correction. With a blog post, you instantly have access to your published content and can edit it as necessary on the spot, providing the most up-to-date information for your business as needed.

Blog responsibilities can be shared out to an entire group (from any department) or be assigned to a single person. Knowledge of the marketplace, the consumers, and the industry will help build a blog's presence online, and so the marketing team is a great place to start.

The marketing department can be vital to a blog's existence, especially in the early days after a blog's creation. Logos, messaging, header images, and branding need to be considered; these are marketing's specialty. These branding elements might differ from existing company standards, as they can be made to look more social media-friendly. So, a customized Twitter logo with the company's username might be used, for example, along with a custom Facebook page icon. You may find that those who are already tasked with getting the business message out, such as those in the marketing department, will be willing to work on a blog. The blog will complement and evolve their existing messaging and tailor it to an online-specific audience. Again, your marketing department is the first place to look!

Client Services and Tech Support

Search engines such as Google are becoming the "go-to" when people need information about something. Therefore, a blog that's searchable (and findable) will lead those seeking information about your industry/products directly to your site. Remember, too, that you can leverage client services skills on your blog; they already know how to converse with customers. These professionals will quickly understand how to moderate comments and publish concise and comprehensible posts. Client services can provide answers to frequently asked questions or perhaps contribute content about product care and maintenance.

You might not want to burden existing staff with additional tasks (such as writing a blog post), but you do want their valuable input. If you have a Director of Social Media in place or a team of authors, these people should reach out to the existing staff to help target messaging.

When creating content for a site, the blog's manager can contact client services to find out common customer queries. Each of these is fuel for a blog post. Such blog posts then provide answers to readers before they even ask for the questions (at least in this forum).

If your company provides forms or documents online, you may want to post about how to properly fill those out. If you have an accounting firm, you can post tax tips for individuals or how to contact the IRS. If your business cleans gutters, you can post about how to keep leaves from clogging drains.

Such customer assistance provided in blog posts doesn't take business away from your company. Instead, it shows that your business cares about educating its customers and making sure they have all the pertinent information necessary to troubleshoot problems before having to escalate the issue.

This subject matter can be collected from the client services department and then composed in a blog post either by the designated author or someone in the department. Remember that you want to convey credibility via the writer's profile. So, for example, a post about how to install a program on your computer written by someone in the supplier's client services department will have more credibility than an anonymous or admin-signed post.

Tech support is also a good department to turn to for blog input. When an issue arises, this department can post updates, and thus allow the blog to become a support resource (without interminable wait times on the phone or at a "genius" bar). As with client services, posts published by writers from tech support will be credible within their domain of expertise. Online updates about services will empower your client base and serve as a selling point for potential customers.

If your company offers a service that requires status updates and support, you can task tech support with updating its own section of the blog. When services go offline, systems go down, or an outage occurs, customers and clients will go online to try to find information about the problem. Your blog can be the home for such critical updates, informing people quickly. Many Web site hosting services provide these status update blogs and services (for example, the microblogging platform Twitter). In August 2009, Twitter was hit with a direct denial-of-service attack that caused the system to stop functioning for millions of users. Fortunately, Twitter had http://status.twitter.com up and running and so could provide updates for users who could not reach the service.

Authentic Content

Business blogs may also feature employees or officers of a company writing about their professional experiences. An example is John Heald, Senior Cruise Director with Carnival Cruise Lines. Although Heald notes on his blog that it is a personal account, he openly discloses his position with Carnival Cruise Lines and discusses all aspects of his life as a cruise director (see Figure 6.2). Heald's blog is promoted and linked from Carnival.com and is also syndicated on Carnival's official "Blogs" page as a resource under the heading "Fun Online."

Figure 6.2 *John Heald's blog, Carnival's Senior Cruise Director.*

If each department does not have time to compose posts, a single coordinator can collect articles written by contributors throughout the company and publish those on the blog. In either case, it is important to remain transparent, noting the original authors and sources of the piece. Ghost writers are not recommended; you don't want readers to feel misled or betrayed. Because audiences online value authenticity, such feelings may lead to social media backlash that can include negative blog posts about the content, negative comments on Twitter, or grassroots online campaigns to dismay others from reading nongenuine content.

Consider the case of a person reading a blog post by the president of a company. That reader then communicates with the president, but only then finds out that the president of the company had nothing to do with the post. That reader will feel betrayed. This sense of betrayal exists because blogs make writers seem personal and approachable, which might not otherwise be the case. Take Oprah, for example. Within the first week of signing up for Twitter, she had more than one million followers. Perhaps people wanted to show her they were fans, or maybe people wanted to see and read updates directly from the talk show host herself. Her name attached to even the most mundane update creates a thrill for those looking to connect with her. Individual messages can be a great way to reach out to audiences from within a company, but you must handle them with care. Note the true author, and be sure to respond in the comments to keep the genuine conversations flowing.

Hiring a Blogger

Sometimes the best person to write a blog is a professional blogger. Blogging has been around for more than ten years now, and many individuals across the globe blog professionally. These bloggers are either experts in their fields, journalist-like in nature, passionate about their subject matter, or resourceful researchers who can put together interesting posts on any topic. A hired blogger can instantly get your company up-to-speed with all the elements involved in managing a blog while allowing you time to consider the content you want to use.

When hiring a blogger, you'll want to become familiar with the blogger's current body of work. Make sure the content she is passionate about and has covered in the past is a good fit. Also make sure that she has not published anything questionable that you wouldn't want linked or brought to your company's blog.

You can ask the blogger about her statistics, such as how many unique visitors a month she has coming to her sites or how she would moderate comments. You can get a feel for an existing online presence by asking what social networks she currently uses and whether she has used these tools in a business capacity before.

Many sites offer advice about hiring bloggers. One such site is Jim Turner's BloggersforHire.com, as shown in Figure 6.3.

Tips for Hiring a Blogger

You could also hire a blogger who does not currently write about your topic, as long as he is willing to immerse himself in your company's industry. You always want someone who can be passionate about the subject matter. If you've found a fabulous blogger who can bring in an audience, spread your message, and get you ranked highly in search engines, you want to also make sure that he can write compelling and interesting content about your company and industry. If he is completely new to your business, you could even disclose that on your blog and have the blogger learn along with the audience.

Figure 6.3 *BloggersforHire.com by Jim Turner.*

For example, a personal blogger was hired to provide new media services to a payment gateway company that handled secure financial transactions online. The company wanted to include a blog in its new media strategy and knew that this blogger could get it on track as the blogger knew the blogging industry. The blogger created the blog, filled in a biography for herself and the company, and began writing her first blog post about the PCI DSS (Payment Card Industry Data Security Standard). This was something that the blogger had never heard of, so in her first blog post she said exactly that, and "let's learn about PCI DSS together." Over the next few weeks, she featured YouTube videos, quotes, and links from other financial blogs with information about the process and the regulation, all while "learning together" with the audience. Within a month, if you searched "PCI Blog" on Google, you would get the blog she had built. The audience knew that she was just learning, but it was able to pick up tips, information, links to useful sites, and also learn about the company she was helping.

Bloggers can be hired to write or to manage your company's social media strategies as a whole, including the blog. But, always make it clear who wrote the blog posts and who is managing the blog. Such transparency not only builds up trust with readers, it also helps them identify the voice of the blog.

Hiring a Blogger from Your Industry

A search for someone who knows the ins and outs of trackbacks, statistics, link tracking, blog terminology, and overall etiquette online combined with personal writing skills may very well lead to hiring a professional blogger. Finding one who already knows the ins and outs of your industry's online audience is a bonus.

If you are in the fruit business, it might be beneficial to approach the top peach blogger to see whether he would like to contribute to your site. If your business is hockey equipment, hire a hockey blogger to talk about what the professionals use or how to keep your skates sharp.

These individuals have dealt with commentary in their respective industries, so they should have an idea about site traffic, and most of all, they are already passionate about the topic. They also know what kind of content gets a response, how to write for an audience, how to use social media tools to expand an audience, and how to track and measure successes. An individual might know all there is to know about computer keyboards, but that doesn't necessarily mean that person knows how to write about them to engage an audience. Much more is involved than just laying out the text of a blog. For example, you'll want to use images and video and reply to comments. An existing industry blogger may be well aware of all of this and would simply need your company's guidance in order to contribute online, on your behalf.

Create a Blogging Position

Director of Social Media positions and such are becoming more common as companies realize that managing all aspects of a corporate blog (and all that comes with it) is often worthy of its own position.

In July 2009, CNN's CareerBuilder.com writer released "Five Jobs for Facebook Addicts," which included a Director of Social Media position. (You can read the other listings at http://www.cnn.com/2009/LIVING/worklife/07/28/cb.best.job. facbook.addict/index.html.)

Social Media Director Requisites and Responsibilities

Companies need someone to manage all aspects of a social media strategy, of which the company blog is one component. The Directory of Social Media oversees the company's entire online presence, tracks statistics, creates partnerships with other bloggers to publicize campaigns, and manages blog content by moderating comments and coming up with the general road map for the company's use of social media.

A person hired for a social media position should know the following:

- How to set the company up with YouTube, including what should be posted there

- How to use Twitter and Facebook and engage with the different audiences on those platforms

- How to reach out to existing customers through the current Web site and introduce them to the blog

- How to get more blog readers, comments, and feedback flowing

- How the company wants to measure success with each one of these strategies

The person in charge of social media for your company should ensure the company is represented online through open, interactive, and personal communications while remaining professional at all times.

The search for your Director of Social Media (or similar role) could be internal if someone in the company already knows the ins and outs of social media. Otherwise, taking to the networks where you would like to see your company have a presence is a great way to find your champion of social media. Publish job postings online, or if you already have a blog, feature the job posting there.

Fitting In with the Company Dynamic

When supporting a blogger who is writing for your company, key messaging can be supplied. However, authors can also do research for their posts, to provide the most informed content for your audience. You can give the author free rein with regard to his or her writing, as long as it pertains to your industry. For example, if you have an Indian restaurant, you could ask the blogger to cover Indian cuisine in general. The blogger could write a post about specific dishes, how they are prepared, where to get the best ingredients and spices in town, and so on.

You can also provide the content on which the blogger will expand. If the company is issuing a press release, information should be given to the blogger so that he can create a post or story pertaining to the news.

Suppose, for example, that you issue a press release about an employee's promotion. In this case, the blogger may want to interview the employee or post a photo (something more personal than the press release but that also complements the same news).

You get to set the rules for your blog. You may allow the blogger to write about specific topics, an industry, or within other specific parameters. To add structure to a site, you may want to impose word counts on posts and consider daily/weekly themes. Such guidelines help ensure that posts stay on topic, and that the blog's author stays within the company's key messaging. You also want to make sure that your bloggers do not overstep boundaries by perhaps sharing personal information about employees or private information about upcoming projects.

Supplying More Than Content

Creating blog posts, managing the online presence (for example, checking out Google Alerts or using Twitter search), moderating comments, analyzing traffic and search terms, posting responses to comments, and researching content are just a few of the tasks that an internal blogger or social media professional can handle.

Professional bloggers should be able to do most of their work after a blog post is written. Once that content is out there, they need to follow up and see just how far of a reach the content had. They can do this using statistics applications and by checking a few of the basics:

- Have there been any comments on the post?

- Has anyone linked/tracked back to your post from their own website?

- Is the post searchable in Google? If so, under which terms does it appear in search results?

- Has it been re-tweeted (that is, your link reposted on Twitter)?

- Has the post appeared yet in your RSS feed? How often do you get new subscribers?

Bloggers also know their audiences by looking at comments and tracking statistics. Should you determine that your blog's traffic is highest midweek during the 9 to 5 hours, you thus understand that your audience is at work and reading during the day. This audience might not be around on the weekends (and therefore the drop in traffic). In this scenario, you don't need to worry about publishing content on the weekend; your audience won't be back until Monday anyway. This is an example of what a good Director of Social Media (with blogging experience) can assess for you.

Advantages of Hiring a Blogger

By having a blogging position, you welcome the blog's author into your company, and by so doing get the best content published. They will have the knowledge required to cover your business, and they will also be personally invested in doing the best job possible. Representing a company online is much easier when you feel at home within the company. The passionate content can then flow much more easily.

Managing a blog and its social media elements can be a full-time job and may be impossible for existing employees to work into their current workload. The blogger will need input from the rest of the departments, however; after all, they are creating and nurturing this online space for the company. The company blogger should clear the way for more involvement, including the possibility of having multiple authors.

The key to finding a professional blogger who is the right fit for your company is to read the writer's blog and get to know her online writing style and behavior. Ideally, you want to find someone who is responsible with online content, courteous to readers, and who hasn't posted material that could embarrass you should that blogger become associated with your company.

One advantage of hiring an experienced blogger is that she should already know the ins and outs of the online realm. This means she should know how to compose a blog post, how to arrange RSS feeds, moderate comments, and publish your links to Twitter or other social networks.

Even those who have only been blogging a short time can still figure out statistics, commenting, and Google searches. Experienced bloggers know how to collect this data and use it to their advantage, tailoring posts and adding keywords to make sure their message gets spread.

Experienced bloggers may already have a presence on multiple online networks or directories and could boost your company's presence there, too. For example, someone who has created Facebook fan pages followed by thousands will know how to boost your presence on that network. That person could also apply those skills to blogging.

There are thousands of professional bloggers in North America, and millions of bloggers worldwide write consistent content online. You can find one for your company by doing blog searches for key terms, checking in on industry bloggers, and listening to what people are already saying about your company online. Sometimes those who are already fans of your company (and who may already have fan-based blogs about your business) can be your biggest asset.

For example, Mike Pegg was a fan of Google Maps and ran the Google Maps Mania Blog (http://googlemapsmania.blogspot.com). He collected stories and images from all over the world and published them online. He ended up on Google's radar, and they then recruited him to work for Google Maps & Earth. (See his bio online at http://www.google.com/profiles/113532747879926407110.) Pegg is now the Product Marketing Manager, Google Maps API, at Google Inc.

Case Study: Linda Bustos: An Elastic Blog from Elastic Path

Linda Bustos is the E-commerce Analyst for professional e-commerce solutions provider Elastic Path. She began her career with the company as a guest blogger for their Get Elastic blog (see Figure 6.4). Elastic Path currently serves more than 200 clients worldwide, including Samsonite and Aeroplan, and they also power the Vancouver 2010 Olympic store.

Figure 6.4 *Get Elastic, The Ecommerce Blog, by Elastic Path.*

In 2006, Bustos began her own blog about social media and SEO (search engine optimization) after attending local news media events in Vancouver, British Columbia. Around the same time, Elastic Path was looking for ways to expand its communications presence online, and so it started up a company blog. Linda soon met Elastic Path's co-founder, Jason Billingsley, at one of these networking events and began checking out Get Elastic because its subject matter was right up her alley.

She often commented and engaged the authors in conversations and was eventually invited to write a guest post. "It wasn't a full-time position in the beginning but just contributing as a guest. After that, there was opportunity to continue full time, as they really wanted to go ahead with the blog."

As the company expanded its blog to provide an industry service, sharing tips and insights about the e-commerce realm, Linda's role began to grow. She was welcomed into the company officially and was included in conversations such as the sales and marketing meetings. These more personal interactions benefited her writing almost immediately. "It really, really helped me to come in and actually learn about the product, and learn about the company," said Bustos. "I think I can help them more with blogging when I keep in mind what their goals are and what they're working on."

Linda's passion for social media, writing, and online marketing truly helped her apply what she knew about the online world and combine it with Elastic Path's endeavors. "They gave me complete flexibility, complete autonomy in what I wanted to write about," noted Bustos, who was able to write passionately about a topic she knew very well. "I try to use the blog as much as possible to build a community around us."

In just over two years, Bustos went from being a guest blogger to being the author of the number one blog in the industry. She offered some advice on how to choose a blogger who will work for your company, recommending that businesses find someone who can be committed, either full- or part-time, to writing and managing the blog.

"If they can't be a full-time employee, at least be a permanent contractor," Bustos noted. "Because on the blog, you definitely don't want to build up trust with one person both internally and with the readership and then swap them out for some-one else." Finding the right blogger for the job and nurturing their messaging is paramount. "It's important that you do your diligence and find somebody who is going to be committed and that can kind of prove themselves as a right fit for the content you want to go with before you have them publishing."

In terms of hiring an external individual to manage your company's blog versus having someone on the inside commit to contributing, Bustos says a hybrid of both can work.

"If I had to choose, I would like somebody who was full-on a part of the team because that's also the trust that you're communicating in a business blog," said Bustos. Having someone on board who can spread your message effectively in the online realm and build up a community of trust with readers and clients is key. Once you find this balance, your company's blog can position you as thought leader in your industry.

Having a game plan in mind when starting up a company blog is always a great idea, because it will serve as a road map and help you plot out goals and strategies. "Be clear about what the game plan is for the blog in terms of keeping a consistent posting schedule," recommended Bustos. With a plan in place, your company will have a road map to plot out goals and milestones for your online communications strategy.

When your company designates a blogger, it is also important to make sure that person is supported. Bustos noted that setting up processes and support for the blog is a great help when it comes to upgrades and technical issues on the back end. This can be internal support or through a contracted partner.

Bustos was passionate about a subject, and because of this she was able to commit to writing and blogging while building an audience. She has helped her company build its readership by being someone who knows the blogging and e-commerce industry. At the same time, she has learned how to share Elastic Path's messaging, and as a result, Get Elastic has been recognized by TopRank as a top search

marketing blog (http://www.toprankblog.com/search-marketing-blogs/),
by the *Wall Street Journal* as one of 15 entrepreneur blogs worth reading
(http://blogs.wsj.com/independentstreet/2008/06/13/15-entrepreneur-blogs-worth-reading), and is on the AdAge Power 150 (http://adage.com/power150/).

Summary

Companies can become overwhelmed with managing a blog, finding where it will
fit in, and writing it. As demonstrated in this chapter, there are plenty of resources
out there to help you get your blog started, whether it's hiring an experienced
blogger or rounding up departmental teams to share the work.

After the blog has an author or authors, the focus should be on content and how to
share that content in a way that it attracts readers. The following chapter details
ways to boost your online presence so that once your blog goes live on your end,
it will also hit the radar of the online audience you hope to bring in as your reader
base.

7

Getting Eyeballs to Your Blog

You may not instantly find readers for your blog within the first few minutes of publishing a post, but there are ways to boost your audience and bring awareness to your writing.

You can add your blog to directory listings or use search engine optimization (SEO) tips so that it is searchable, but when it comes purely to content, you will also need to attract readers who will want to return with each post. Great content that serves to educate, inform, or entertain is the driving force behind building an audience with your blog. This chapter shows you how to get your audience to return your blog.

Writing Effectively

After you get an audience to your site, it's key to provide content that will capture its interest and encourage it to return again with each new post. Effective writing includes the following characteristics:

- **Appropriate length of writing**: You need to learn how to edit your content for appropriate length.

- **A voice or tone that is human**: Your writing needs to be personal.

- **Readable language**: The words you choose are important in that they need to be clear and readable.

Editing for Word Count and Brevity

Effective writing on a blog should not sound like a text message in short code or chat room speak, nor should it sound like an extended press release. It can contain the same key elements of information of both because when you need to get your message across with a limited word count, you make sure to say what you need to say in that space. Learning how to self-edit is key.

When putting blog posts together, you aren't necessarily limited to word counts; however, having a milestone in mind can help you weed out the best information you want to present. Blog posts of about 250 to a maximum of 700 words allow enough room for the content to flow without sounding too choppy or brief while not extending the post so it stretches beyond the readers' attention span.

Write the post, save it, preview it, edit it, and then repeat the process. Editing down your content so that you can publish the most clear and concise information will make your posts easier to read.

Most blog platforms enable you to preview your post before it is published, and you should preview your article before making the post public. You can preview your post and also read through it several times to make sure you can get the most pertinent information included before losing the reader to a long word count. Setting a word count goal often helps authors keep their posts as clear and concise as possible.

With the growing popularity of microblogging sites such as Twitter, people are finding more ways to cram as much information they can into a strict and often very short character limit. It's amazing to see what you can produce when given guidelines like these.

One of Technorati's Top 100 blogs, Boing Boing is a hub of information, photos, videos, and links to cool sites across the Internet. Blog posts about the world's smallest robots show an image, a quick blurb, and a link to the Web site where the content is posted. When their authors are excited about a new film that is about to launch, they'll post an embedded YouTube video, some text about the film, and a link to the film's website for more information.

These short yet helpful posts provide multiple forms of content while also leading to discussion in the comments. When your post is brief, it's easy to expand on its content through reader feedback. Even though your entry may be but 200 words, your interaction with readers in the comments help continue your thoughts while at the same time showing readers you would like to hear their thoughts, too.

In April 2008, the popular photo-sharing site Flickr began allowing its pro users to upload and share videos, as well. They decided to put restrictions on those videos, allowing clips that were no longer than 90 seconds or no larger than 150MB in size. The 90-second limit never ended up being an issue for users because most video clips on the Web these days are 90 seconds or shorter. Anything more and you risk losing the audience's attention or becoming a full Web series or episode rather than a video clip.

The same applies for blog posts. There should be an element of brevity, but at the same time you should still be able to fit all necessary information in the post. Also, if blog authors look at their Web site's statistics, they should see a Bounce Rate section. This tells you how long readers are staying on your blog before heading to another Web site. Typical bounce rates are anywhere between 60 and 90 seconds, which means you only have a short time to grab the reader's attention, and keep it locked on your blog.

Problogger answered the question, "How Long Should a Blog Post Be?" in 2006 by looking at the following issues:

- **Reader attention span**: Once again, attention to the "bounce rate" or how long you can keep a reader captivated by your content.

- **SEO**: Search engine optimization refers to making sure that your blog and its contents are going to be picked up by search engines through keywords and other elements. According to Problogger, extremely short posts and those that are extremely long have a hard time being picked up by search engines. The suggested blog post length is between 250 and 1,000 words.

- **Number of posts**: Having shorter posts allows you to write more often, because it shouldn't take as long to write a 300-word post compared to one that is 1,200 words. By doing so, your search engine ranking can improve (based on the previous item) and you'll pull readers back to your blog more often with fresh content.

Read the full post on Problogger at http://www.problogger.net/archives/ 2006/02/18/post-length-how-long-should-a-blog-post-be.

A great resource for checking the reading level of your site is http://readability.info. You can use this Web site to determine how "readable" your content is. According to Readability.info, a typical *New York Times* article has a fifth grade reading level, whereas *PC World* is at an eighth grade level. A professional blog that is between these levels will be quick and easy to read while still providing knowledge and insight.

Blog posts don't need to always include text. Posts can take on many forms and may be as quick and simple as an embedded video with a caption or an entire gallery of photos from an event or product launch. Choose multimedia that is relevant (for example, using images to illustrate an object or place). Visual aids help the reader get a better idea of what you're talking about in a post, and they also break up chunks of text. If the images or video are not your own, because you can source these from networks like Flickr or YouTube, be sure to always give credit by linking to your original sources online.

Be Human

The corporate and company blog connects with readers, clients, and your audience on a personal level, so writing in that exact manner is paramount. When writing for a blog, losing sentence structure and grammar is not an option; however, you'll want to make sure your posts have a voice and can connect with readers on a familiar and friendly level.

An individual or group of individuals should write company blogs. You can set your blog's preferences to display author names, which can help create that voice, or set a more personal tone. Reading a post from Administrator is not as personal as one from Jennifer in Marketing, especially when it pertains to a specific aspect of the company.

A good example is the Disney Parks Blog (http://disneyparks.disney.go.com/blog/), which does not speak down to readers although most of its audience worldwide consists of children. The blog provides an inside look at the Disney parks, including individual items of note that readers might not already know. These insights include blog posts about how you can burn 350 calories an hour by walking briskly from *land* to *land*, a feature about dishes you should try at the Epcot International Food & Wine Festival, or an announcement about their handheld audio devices which now play descriptions of the attractions.

Other authors on the blog include Thomas Smith, the Social Media Director of Disney Parks; however, having a blog post about "Cinderella's Coach for Disney Weddings" written by the company's wedding specialist gives it context and more of a human element. Each post is also professional and informative while still using the author's own voice.

Another example is the official Google Blog (http://googleblog.blogspot.com), which also has many authors who all contribute to the same site. At the end of each post, each author clearly states who wrote the post, and each one's job title is displayed. For example, you can read a post about Google's translation services, written by Jeff Chin, a Product Manager.

Adding these personal touches boosts the credibility of your posts. Who better to inform you about Google's Open Source initiatives in a blog post than Leslie Hawthorn, Program Manager of the Open Source Team? The author can have a biography on the side of your blog, at the bottom of each post, or on a separate About This Blog page. This will help readers connect with a specific person at the company and the blog as a whole, enabling the audience to connect with a human.

The blog is not the place for a press release or similar verbiage, either. Should your company disseminate a release, feel free to link that information or include it in a post; however, its entire contents should not be included. The blog should be conversational and encourage discussions. It's also a great place to include photos or accompanying multimedia that helps assignment editors, readers, and journalists get even more information from the company.

Through accompanying images or videos supplied on the blog, more can be shared and your message can reach a wider audience through photo- or video-sharing networks. Readers might not be interested in an image of a new product but a fun video posted to YouTube might catch their attention.

Be Readable

In the digital age, attention spans are slim, and multimedia captures more eyeballs than blocks of text. When composing blog posts, beware of your word counts and try to break up large chunks of text on the screen with images, logos, icons, or video embeds. Keeping the readers' attention is as simple as writing content that gets straight to the point and leaves them wanting more, whether by coming back to check out the next post or by leaving a comment to continue the discussion with the author.

Design

Web site design also has a lot to do with being readable. As noted previously, up-to-date content also attracts readers so your latest content should be at the top of your blog. If your most recent post is from two months ago, a reader may not become engaged with your site knowing that it is not current. An effective blogger should write a new post at least once a week.

Blog layouts should feature your core content by displaying it in the clearest manner possible. Your post content should fit nicely on your blog layout without expanding too far across the page, causing readers to scroll left to right. Content can also be presented alongside an image or thumbnail so that the text is broken up, making it easier on the eyes than a single block of text.

Tiled image backgrounds, faint yellow text on a white background, or colors that are too bright may turn readers off your content before they get a chance to read it.

Choosing colors for your blog that complement its theme, design, or your corporate branding can ensure a consistent design. If you have a black blog background, white is probably your best bet for clarity, and readability; the opposite then applies to a blog with a white background. Contrasting colors make the text easier to read (see Figure 7.1). You also want to choose a typeface that is easy to read, such as a sans-serif font, as opposed to something cursive.

Figure 7.1   *Choosing a font and color scheme that is easy to read, and easy on the eyes.*

Make sure your hyperlinks are underlined, bold, or a slightly different shade of font color. Your readers will immediately know when text is linked if it is displayed in this manner. You can also configure your design to have hyperlinked text or images change slightly when hovered over by the reader's cursor.

Read other blogs to help you write yours. You can use any of your favorite blogs as reference points. Determine what designs or layouts are most enjoyable for you to read and go from there on your own site. We discuss this later in the chapter but doing online searches for blogs that contain keywords that interest you is a good way to start finding favorites.

Reading Blogs Helps You Write Blogs

When deciding to write a blog, the best way to find out what to write and how to write it is by seeking out blogs that you like to read. What keeps your attention? What content-styles are the most appealing to you? By reading successful sites, you can collect valuable publishing ideas that can be easily applied to your own blog venture.

Commenting: More than Leaving a Calling Card

According to Technorati's State of the Blogosphere 2008 (http://technorati.com/blogging/state-of-the-blogosphere/the-how-of-blogging), 77 percent of bloggers attract readers by commenting on other blogs.

If you read an interesting blog post on another Web site, it's perfectly acceptable to join the conversation in the comment thread. Leaving comments on any other blog will show other readers that you are active in the industry blogging community, you have ideas and thoughts to share, and doing so will hopefully lead readers back to your site to see your expanded insights.

However, when commenting on other sites, remain tactful in your message. Only leave a comment when you genuinely have an interest in the post and can contribute something productive. Simply leaving a link to your site and saying you also wrote about a certain topic can easily get your comment flagged as spam. When you share information and encourage others to do the same on your blog with your own posts, it creates a respectful blogging community for your industry within which you'll be a key player.

You can also see how others respond to posts and comments, seeing what works for other blogs, and what doesn't in terms of connecting with an audience. If you notice that you start getting more comments on posts about a particular topic, continue writing about that topic in more entries.

Blogger Outreach

Approaching other bloggers, whether they are in your industry or a fan of products and services pertaining to your industry, can also be mutually beneficial. Going beyond a simple link back to a preferred blog, you can even approach these writers when you have a campaign to promote, an event, or perhaps even for a guest blog post.

Professional bloggers live all across the Internet, and chances are, some cover your industry on a daily basis. Feel free to add these bloggers to mailing lists, or visit their sites to touch base. Once again, the importance of "being human" and personable is key in these communications. E-mailing full press releases to a blogger might be an instant turn off. However, if you read their site, get a feel for their coverage and writing style, you can send them a personalized note if you think they would be genuinely interested in your news. Getting picked up on their site could drive some valuable traffic your way, and in exchange, they get to cover your interesting news.

Product launch parties and even press trips are organized for bloggers in the hopes that companies will get applicable coverage online. For example, in the summer of 2009, Coast Hotels & Resorts invited six bloggers from the Vancouver area over to Victoria, the capital of British Columbia, on Vancouver Island. The idea was to highlight the quick trip from Vancouver to the island and feature restaurants, businesses, and activities in the greater Victoria region. The blogger guest list consisted of travel bloggers, food bloggers, and photographers. Coast Hotels sponsored the bloggers' stay in Victoria and hooked them up with Tourism Victoria so that they could explore the city. In no way were any of the bloggers obliged to write about Coast Hotels, or even any of their experiences. However, Coast did provide the bloggers with multimedia (images from the Royal BC Museum, a menu from featured restaurants where they ate, and so on) and they even created a hashtag on Twitter, #newvictoria.

Note

Hashtags allow readers of a specific following to track topics on Twitter. Placing a hashtag, or pound sign, next to a word allows others to click through and follow all instances of that word or topic using http://search. twitter.com. A great example is at a conference called AB Conference. All attendees could include #ABConference in their tweets about the event so that everyone (in attendance and at home) can follow the flow of information online.

Throughout their stay, bloggers can tweet, blog, and post content about their experiences while Coast could track their messages using the tags they had set up. By the end of the weekend, almost 1,000 photos were uploaded to Flickr, which were all tagged "new Victoria" and the bloggers also used "Coast Hotels."

Providing bloggers with links to a Flickr group, where they can submit their own images to a community pool of photos, and a hashtag enabled Coast to track the content that was created.

The same applies to hosting an event or a product launch party. Provide the Twitter hashtag, a link to your blog post about the event, and a place for bloggers to find images (or upload their own), and then facilitate content creation by not demanding it.

If you're open to inviting mainstream media, also consider bloggers who cover your industry. Their audiences are even more specific and may be those you most want to reach. You can offer them access and any other event benefits, and in turn they might write about it on their site (and perhaps even include photos).

The opportunity to write a guest blog post for your blog may also appeal to bloggers who cover your industry, or even to your readers within the same industry. Bloggers get added exposure and the prestige of writing professionally for your site, and in exchange, they will link and promote their article on their own outlet. Each option provides links, promotion, and visibility to both blogs and businesses.

LinkedIn, one of the world's top professional social networking sites, runs the LinkedIn Blog (http://blog.linkedin.com). Multiple authors post about everything from small business to networking tips. They run a blog series called Success Stories for which they welcome guest posts from LinkedIn users. The series is searchable through a category tag (http://blog.linkedin.com/category/success-stories), and each guest author is given a biography at the top of each post that includes a link to their own Web site. The Success Stories series not only gives users a chance to provide feedback, but it also encourages readers to use the LinkedIn service based on the positive outcomes that are highlighted.

Linking Out to Get Incoming Links

Getting an idea of what your industry is currently doing in the online space is a great way to put together your own blogging plan. One of the best ways to become a part of the blogging community in your industry is by becoming active on other sites, and perhaps even linking to them from your blog. Linking out to your competition might seem like a silly idea, but it's just another step in becoming a total resource for your clients and audience.

When you read an interesting post or article online, you can copy and paste the link into your own blog post, attaching it to reference text. For example, "I read an interesting post about the new MP3 players over on ABC Company's blog [link]." You can even include some of their post's text as long as you are sure to reference it and include a link back to the original source.

Finding the link is as easy as looking in your browser's address bar and copying the blog post's address. After you have copied that code, you can highlight your text, and in most blogging platforms, you can click the link button to paste in the code you just copied.

After you have included a link in your post, the original site author will be able to see this incoming link using her own statistics applications.

Because most blogs have systems in place to track statistics, incoming links are a metric that are often closely watched. It's always fun to get quoted or linked in someone else's blog post, so providing links and credit on your site to others can help this chain continue.

Search Engine Optimization

Search engines each have their own specific algorithms for what content they pick up and place in their results. By having good search engine optimization, or SEO, your blog can get readers with little effort.

Search engines look for keywords and key content when scouring your blog posts for content they can index and call up in their search results. Keywords in the title of a blog post, the title of a blog page, and in the link structure can help boost your SEO.

For example, if your blog post is about a new brand of jeans, it would be useful to include those keywords in your post's title (for example, "New Bootcut Jeans Released this Winter"). Titles should be keyword-rich but still make sense and per-tain to the post's content. Search engines can also penalize a site (refusing to include it in results) if it is clearly milking keywords that are irrelevant. It may seem poetic to name a blog post after a song lyric, but if you're looking to drive traffic to the content, using keywords in the title is much more effective.

Blogrolls

If you want to become a one-stop resource for your company's online presence and your industry, providing the most information and media for your audience should include a blogroll. A *blogroll* is a list of links to Web sites that you would like to share with your readers. These can be other blogs from your company, blogs from your industry, or simply links to blogs that you find interesting.

As with linking out in a blog post, other blogs can see links coming from blogrolls using their statistics tracking applications. These applications provide data on traffic sources to your blog; sources can be blog posts, search engines, or other blogrolls.

For other blog authors, it may be considered a compliment or sign of prestige if they are linked off of a reputable company blog in a blogroll. If you have a favorite blog or find other blogs you think your readers would enjoy, you can show your appreciation to that blog's author by linking to them.

The Check Out blog (see Figure 7.2), the official gadget blog of Wal-Mart and Sam's Club, provides a blogroll on their main page that links to other gadget and technology-related blogs.

By coming to the Check Out blog, readers are also treated to a list of sites where they can find useful information. They might click through and read a gadget review on another site, and then come back to Wal-Mart online to make their purchase. It's not a guarantee, but if your site can provide useful information, including links to other sites with comprehensive data and reviews, you could find reader loyalty there, which can translate to customer loyalty.

Linking to Other Blog Posts

Reading other blog posts to get ideas for articles of your own is a great way to build content on your site, as mentioned earlier in the section "Linking Out to Get Incoming Links." If you see a post elsewhere that is worth quoting or expanding upon on your own site, be sure to copy only a portion of the post and provide a link back to the source, crediting the author. This courtesy goes a long way when it comes to blogging etiquette. The original author will see your link, and may come over to your site to see your additional thoughts.

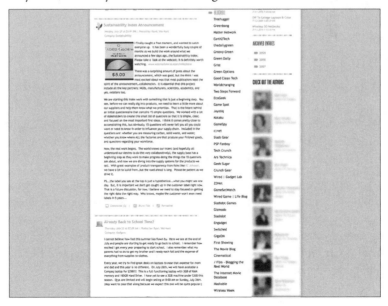

Figure 7.2   *The Check Out blog's blogroll of other gadget and technology blogs.*

You will at least get the original author to view your post. If they have a trackback system in place, where your link shows up as a comment on their blog post, your post will be linked from the original post automatically. With your link now on their post, you'll attract readers from the original source's site because they may want to see how you have continued the conversation or why you have linked that post.

If your thoughts on a particular blog post expand beyond just leaving a comment for another blogger, you can create your own post inspired by the original. Mention that you read about the topic on the source's site, and expand your thoughts on your own post. If linked correctly, you will get the trackback on your post showing up on theirs. This allows the discussion to continue on your site, alongside your own thoughts and productive/relative notes.

When linking out, do so for good reason and be sure to link appropriately. Your post should expand on theirs or have something to do with the content to which you are linking. If there is no relevance, your attempt at linking out to draw links back in could be seen as spam. By being courteous, adding to a conversation or simply highlighting something great that you read, you'll attract positive attention and hopefully new readers.

Write Interesting Content

You can include keywords, links, and write as many readable blog posts as you like, but if your content isn't interesting, you won't have people to read what you are publishing.

Highlight Industry Players

Profiling some of your favorite blogs is a great way to showcase your involvement in blogging and maintain your blog's profile as an industry resource. Should your company be in the restaurant business, an interview with an executive chef could attract readers. If your business is bicycles, an interview with a rider or manufacturer could be of great interest to your readers.

Interviews are always a good way to change up the flow of content on your site and depending on your subject, the rich keywords and tags associated with their names could boost your blog's SEO significantly. You could interview someone who writes a blog, an individual who has expertise in your industry or field, or even do a customer or client profile. As a result, fans of your interview subject will come to your site, ultimately expanding your own audience.

You can also highlight other bloggers within your industry. Britain's Times Online is a Web version of its print publication. Its unique Web content contains blogs and also blogger profiles. In their "Real Food" section, they have a series called "Meet the Food Bloggers" where they highlight food bloggers from across the globe (see Figure 7.3; http://www.timesonline.co.uk/tol/life_and_style/food_and_drink/real_food/).

They have featured and interviewed Seattle's Not Without Salt blog (http://www.notwithoutsalt.com) and Bavaria's Delicious Days blog (http://www.deliciousdays.com). Profiling these top food blogs helps bring traffic in to the publication online and gain an international readership in the process.

In February 2009, the Times Online also published "50 of the World's Best Food Bloggers" (http://www.timesonline.co.uk/tol/life_and_style/food_and_drink/real_food/article5561425.ece). This list drove traffic to the Times Online blogs, for readers who may not have already known about their online presence. Each of the 50 blogs no doubt publicized their placement or involvement with the list.

Figure 7.3   *Meet the Food Bloggers series on Times Online.*

Company Profiles

Businesses should be proud of their employees, from the management team down to part-timers and interns. Showcasing your team members in blog posts is a fun way to introduce your audience to your company in a more personal manner and it shows that you truly value your team. Highlighting employees or departments proves that you not only care about your customers and clients, but those who help make your company work from the inside-out are just as valued. This can be a nice morale booster and a chance for your company to truly shine in your industry.

The outdoor clothing company Patagonia hosts a blog called The Cleanest Line (http://www.thecleanestline.com). They describe the blog as "Weblog for the employees, friends, and customers of the outdoor clothing company Patagonia. Visit Patagonia.com to see what we do."

Because they are all about the outdoors, they occasionally ask employees to share their experiences from their own hikes and adventures in the open air. In the summer of 2009, the managers of the blog caught wind that one of Patagonia's customer service representatives, Adam Bradley, would be doing the Pacific Crest Trail. They then asked him to share thoughts and photos from his journey on their group blog (see Figure 7.4).

A feature like this not only engages employees and gives advice to those who would also like to venture across the Pacific Crest Trail, but it also shows that employees of this outdoor clothing company actually do spend time out in the open air.

Figure 7.4   *The Cleanest Line: Weblog for the employees, friends, and customers of the outdoor clothing company Patagonia.*

Case Study: Vancouver Opera

The Vancouver Opera began blogging in 2008, as they knew they wanted to get into the social media space. They approached Ling Chan, who at the time was the Assistant to the Managing Director, to set up, write, and manage the blog. Chan, now the Social Media Coordinator, was already a personal blogger and was the immediate choice for the organization. She set up the blog using Google's Blogspot blogging platform, and it is currently linked from the main page of the Vancouver Opera Web site at http://vancouveropera.ca (http://vancouveropera.blogspot.com). Chan said that she approached the Opera's blog with great enthusiasm.

During the 2008–2009 season, the Vancouver Opera saw increased interest due to its wide social media presence. "I love opera, and I love the pop culture tie-ins, so it's very easy for me to find things to write about." Chan noted that each blog post starts off with a simple idea and then is researched with care.

"The blog then grew to a place where we could have a new theme each day. Mondays feature opera videos, Tuesdays are trivia, etc." Research for their themes or weekly series includes seeking out the top 10 haunted opera houses in North America or even the top 10 science fiction movies that could be made into operas. The weekly Operamania blog posts appear each Wednesday (see Figure 7.5).

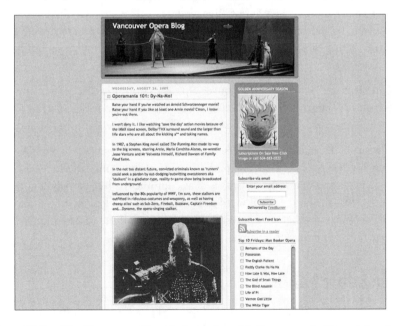

Figure 7.5   *The Vancouver Opera's themed weekly Operamania blog post series.*

However, the traditional opera audience is not necessarily composed of those who are also into social media or blogging. "We promoted it through our Web site, word of mouth, and Facebook. It just grew from there." Chan also says that the new generation of opera goers is finding them online, "just as often as the hardcore opera lovers."

Along with setting up a blog, finding a passionate writer, and promoting the blog, the Vancouver Opera also created Blogger Night at the Opera. For the first time, they opened up the opera to established bloggers from Vancouver who had never experienced the opera before to live blog their experiences from the theater. "We approached these bloggers who were first time opera goers because their experiences at the opera would appeal to our opera (curious or new to opera) readers." For the 2008–2009 opera season, Chan set the bloggers up in the lobby along with signage displaying their blog URLs, supplying them with wireless Internet. Before the opera and between acts, the bloggers could then come out to their table and record their experiences.

Chan also started a photo series on Flickr and Facebook that she called Fashion at the Opera. She takes photos of willing participants before the opera and during intermission, and then posts their images online. The public can comment, add tags, or add their own photos to the Vancouver Opera Flickr group. The bloggers could also use these images in their live blog posts. The Blogger Night at the Opera events were so successful that Chan had other opera companies from around North America calling to ask how to organize their own, and also how to set up their own blogs.

To complement the blog, the Vancouver Opera also set up a Twitter account and offered specials during the season. Through Twitter, they ran BOGO (Buy One Get One free) campaigns and noticed an increase in sales, directly from the updates.

Going forward, Chan already has comments from those wanting to attend a show during the next opera season. She plans to continue blogging, offering weekly themed posts and online specials, as well as continue the Blogger Night at the Opera events. She has her own word of advice for opera blogging in particular: "Write about things that are interesting to both you and the community. Make sure to have fun with it and be creative."

Being Searchable

As previously mentioned, SEO is a hot topic and much sought-after resource for bloggers and Web site managers alike. A Web site that comes up in search results for your targeted industry keywords is extremely valuable. This allows those who are not already aware of your company and blog to discover your resources.

With some blogging platforms, most of your SEO is already taken care of in the way that the system publishes your content and pushes its keywords out to search engines. However, it's beneficial to make sure your blog is optimally set up for these search engines.

To ensure that your blog will get picked up by sites such as Google and Yahoo! Search, you can proactively submit your blog to their directory. With Yahoo!, you can visit their directory listings site to request to be added (https://ecom.yahoo. com/dir/reference/instructions), and with Google, you can also submit your link for their consideration (see Figure 7.6).

Check Your Current Rank

A great first step to working on your SEO is doing a current search for your company name, a post title, or a product/service your business offers.

You can check out your current ranking by going to Grader.com (http://www. grader.com) and clicking on Website.Grader.com. This analytical tool will let you know your current search engine ranking, Google page rank, and a few other helpful details. From there, you can take steps to improve your results.

You can also give your blog results a push by using Google's Webmaster tools (https://www.google.com/webmasters/tools/home?hl=en). Google will allow you to submit your blog and will generate a list of top search queries that led users to your site, along with incoming links, and other useful information.

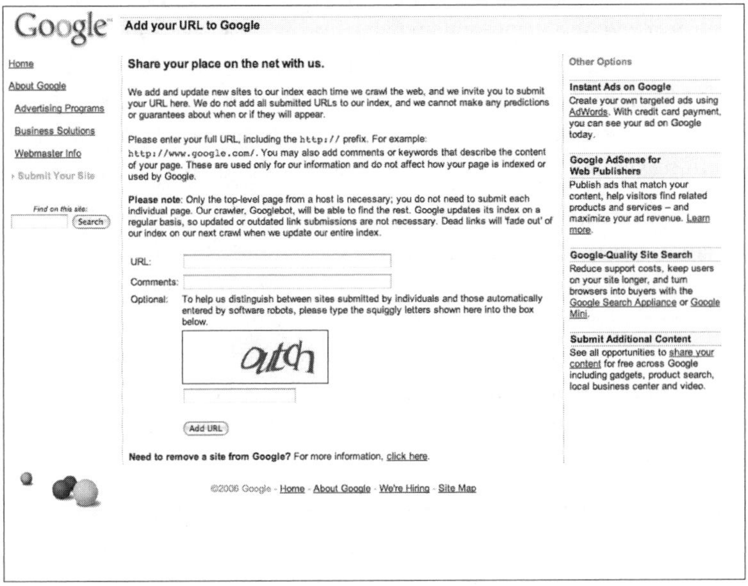

Figure 7.6   *AddURL service from Google.com.*

Clean URLs

URLs are your blog's unique Web site address or link. A clean URL contains actual words that apply to the content. Because Web site addresses are one of the first things crawled by search engines when including your site in their rankings and results, clean URLs can be beneficial. For example, a blog with an address of http://yourcompany.com/?1234 will be less likely to come up in a result as http://yourcompany.com/blog. For individual posts, say one about high heel shoes, the URL should come out as any variation of http://yourcompany.com/blog/latest-high-heel-styles instead of http://yourcompany.com/?1234. Having the keywords directly in the link means you have clean URLs set up on your blog, which means search engines will be able to scan your site with ease.

This feature does not come standard with all blogger platforms. It may be as simple as a setting in your blog's configuration if you are using a popular blogging platform. However, if it is not already standard, you might have to take a few more technical steps behind the scenes to get these in place on your blog.

Keywords and Tags

A distinguishing element of a blog versus a regular Web site is the ability to add tags or categories to posts. Using tags or categories is similar to sorting files into folders. Should you apply a tag called *events* to a blog post, you will then be able to search your blog for all posts you have tagged with *events*. Posts with similar tags are grouped so that you can sort and find them at a later point in time. Your blogging platform will be able present all tagged items on a page and can also provide you with an RSS feed for each. Categories and tags should be keywords that are associated with the content in the blog post. If the blog post is about a fundraising event in Seattle, you could apply the categories or tags *event, fundraiser,* and *Seattle*. In the future, you will be able to search for a post based on any of those keywords.

If your blogging platform provides the option for both categories and tags (they serve a similar purpose), you can treat them differently. Categories can be used at a higher level or more general form of sorting. You could have a category that pertains to all news items, while tagging news items with specific keywords. For example, a blog post could be in the category *News* but also have the tag *product announcement*. Categories and tags are also assigned their own URLs or Web site addresses. This allows you to further sort your content or provide links to an entire range of posts rather than a single item.

These keywords serve a dual purpose in that they sort your content and also make it more searchable. Once again, using the high heel shoe example, http://yourcompany.com/blog/tags/shoes is much more likely to get picked by search engines because the tag name is listed directly in the Web site address. You can also include coded HTML tags when you embed links, photos, and video. This bit of code lets the search engine crawler know exactly what type of content is supplied.

Including the keyword in the title of the multimedia is a quick way to get picked up, too. For example, an uploaded photo called DSC1234.jpg will not get picked up as easily as Stilettos.jpg.

Search engines also look for title information in blog posts. So, when you are naming your articles, include the keywords directly in the title field. However, remember to keep your site readable and "human" sounding by avoiding keyword overload. A title of "Shoes High Heels" might get you some great rankings, but it tells your readers nothing specific about the post. A title such as this may not lead them to your site from the search results to read more. However, including the keywords and keeping the theme of the post within the title should accomplish the click-through (for example, "The Season's Hottest High Heel Shoes").

Promotion

Launching a blog is a newsworthy and notable event for any business. Some companies include this in a press release, and others host launch parties to celebrate the addition to their online presence. Whatever way you plan to launch and promote your blog, the most important thing to do is let people know it exists in the first place. Linking to your blog from your main Web site is the natural place to start, but you can also use your current publicity resources to drive traffic to your blog.

Social Media Networks

Blog promotion can be done through other social media networks. If you already have a Facebook page, posting an announcement there is an obvious decision. The same applies for Twitter or any other social networking service you use. These sites most likely contain the audience you will be looking to nurture on your blog, moving conversations from external sites to your very own.

Announcing Your Blog Launch to Other Communities

You can also reach out to your local or industry blogging communities. In doing so, ask for feedback and be open to suggestions and comments. Be sure to be personal and get a real sense of the blog that you are approaching. If the blog is written by a single male, the author might not be the best person to contact about your new line of baby bottles.

When approaching a blogger by e-mail, be sure to know the author's name and address him as such. You can also reference recent posts they have written or even a favorite of yours, if you have been following their site. Look around on the blog to see whether you think they will in fact be open to sharing your story. (For example, have they written reviews or news articles before?) You also need to make sure the blog isn't questionable in terms of content and that it's not the sort of site your company wouldn't like to be associated with online.

Target Your Newsletter Members

Sending e-mail blasts to your newsletter distribution lists can also bring traffic in to discover your blog. A great way to add more to a newsletter is to link to your blog and expand on topics back over on your blog. This is one way to convert your current audience from an e-mail blast to a more permanent home on your blog. Services like FeedBurner can even convert your blog posts into digest-type e-mails that can be sent to your distribution lists.

By reaching out to an already established and dedicated e-mail audience, you can bring them in as readers of your Web site with these links. If your blog is the best source for your company news or if you sell advertising on your site, you'll want to pull in the largest audience possible. In an age when e-mails fill up inboxes fast and furiously, you could easily convert e-mail subscribers into RSS subscribers or daily blog readers.

Your newsletter or e-mail blast subscribers would still be receiving your content; now they'll just have more options for how they go about reading it.

Press Releases

Launching a blog is a big deal for any business. It's a progressive step toward expanding an online presence and offering rich, informative, and useful content to clients and potential customers. You should treat the blog as an important advertising and communications tool, and a press release is a great way to initially drive traffic in. Not only will recipients see the link, but if the release is picked up on any online news outlet, the link there may boost your blog's search engine ranking.

Online newswire services such as PRWeb, PRNewswire, and traditional newswire services such as Marketwire currently offer social media press release formatting. With this format, you can include links in your press release, online photos, and even embed YouTube videos to enhance your news. Linking to your blog is always a great idea so that those who enjoy your news through this method will now know they can get daily updates from your company through your blog.

Summary

Although there is much involved with bringing readers to your blog, just as much effort needs to go into keeping them there. Returning readers become the foundation of your blog's community. You can achieve this by having easy-to-read content that is informative, educational, or purely entertaining. On top of supplying great content, you need to work at getting the word out through various mediums so that you can continue to grow your readership. There are tips, tools, and tricks out there to promote your efforts and really get your company blog noticed that all involve a dedication to two-way online communications.

8

Getting Interactive with Multimedia Blogging

Blogging doesn't always have to be purely about text. With the use of images, audio, and video, you can enhance any blog post. Images help break up text and provide visuals for a story or news item. Some blog posts could consist of images only or an image gallery about a particular place or product. With photo-sharing services such as Flickr, you can also pull user-generated images in your blog posts. On Flickr, you can search for photos based on tags. So, if you want to include photos from Washington on your blog post, you can search for applicable public images to include.

The use of audio in a blog post is a bit more tricky because it involves more than copying and pasting or uploading a photo. However, audio clips can add context to an interview, for example, enabling readers to read and listen to the original conversations.

Videos are a fun way to enhance your posts. And as with images, you can create a blog post that consists of an embedded video only. Should your company have a new commercial or informative video, blog text can introduce the piece that can be embedded in the post.

All of these methods help give your readers more ways to interact with you on your site. They can click through and comment on photos or video and also be introduced to your other online presences, should you have a video or photo network account. In this chapter, you find even more ways to connect and interact with your audience using all of these multimedia tools.

Offering Multiple Forms of Content

Being an online medium, blogging can be enhanced with multimedia, such as videos, photos, and audio. Bringing these elements into your blog page or blog posts can offer your audience a wide range of information, education, and entertainment. When this multimedia is available for them to share with their own audiences (for example, through an embeddable YouTube video), your message instantly has a wider reach.

Content for All

Content on your blog should always be available to everyone, either on your blog posts, through subscribing, or through a social network that you are tying into your blog. This can include Twitter updates, Flickr photos, audio interviews, podcasts, or videos on a video-sharing network.

As previously mentioned, these forms of content can complement your work, but it is also important to allow others to use them in their works (with attribution/a credit link back to your source).

The benefit of having content that others can share is that your readers or audience can take your information and share it across their networks. For example, Flickr has licenses, and podcasts are available on iTunes via subscription.

Your blog is also a gateway to all of your company's other online presences, such as a Facebook page or a Twitter account. You may have some readers who do not look at blogs often, but they are active on YouTube. By having a YouTube channel, you can reach out to those readers. By promoting your YouTube channel on your blog or including embedded videos, you can let readers know they can also follow you on that network.

By making your videos available and embeddable to the public, your content can get blogged on someone else's site, and your audience may then increase exponentially. The value of this public content on your blog and on multimedia networks is that what you create becomes shareable by others.

Images

Flickr is an online photo-sharing network that enables users to upload photos (or short video clips), use tags to sort them, share them through embeddable links, or group them with other users' photos. You can sign up for a free Flickr account, which has a monthly limit on the number of photos you can upload, or you can go with a Flickr Pro option. Flickr Pro accounts have an affordable annual fee ($24.95 as of November 2009) that gives you unlimited access and resources.

On Flickr, you can sort your photos into sets, which are like online albums. A set can include images from a specific event, about a specific product, or about a particular aspect of a company. Sorting and tagging your images enables other users on the network, and even public users, to find your photos when doing a search on Flickr or on the Web. All Flickr images marked as public also get picked up by search engines, provided the titles include appropriate keywords.

Businesses can also set up groups on Flickr, and thus enable other Flickr users to add or submit images. Lululemon Athletica Inc., an athletic apparel company, has its own Flickr account.

The company posts photos that are filed away in sets. Their sets include photos featuring their latest garments (see Figure 8.1) and events such as a warehouse sale in Hamilton, Ontario, or group yoga in Bryant Park.

Lululemon also created a public group on Flickr (http://www.flickr.com/groups/883166@N20/) that encourages "Lululemon Lovers" to submit their own yoga-wear photos. Flickr users who join the group can submit their photos, which will then appear in the group's image pool. This group image pool can then be embedded into a blog post using the "slideshow" feature on Flickr.

Keywords and Titles

You also want to make sure your images benefit your blog posts by not only looking great but also by providing extra content behind the scenes. This means that in the code that makes up your blog post, you can include special text that will help with your search engine optimization. For example, when you add an image to a blog post, you can include an *alt* or *title* tag. These are just extra bits of code that search engines look for when adding your site to their directory listings. Most blogging platforms ask you for the image's title when you are uploading; these can also be added using HTML code.

Figure 8.1 *Lululemon on Flickr: Fit & Function: Embark Softshell II photo set.*

If you are using an HTML composer, add *alt="keyword text"* within the image code so that the image code will appear as follows:

```
<img src=http://yoursite.com/image.jpg alt="eating ice cream in the
park">.
```

The result of this code is an embedded view of image.jpg. However, when you hover your cursor over the image, you'll be able to read "eating ice cream in the park." This extra bit of information is also useful for the visually impaired who are browsing the Web. Audio reading tools can provide them with the text of the post, but when an image is included, that doesn't translate well into audio. Title tags included with your image allow them to *hear* the image in your post as "eating ice cream in the park" rather than "image123.jpg."

Having the *alt* or *title* text allows search engines to pick up on your extra content through the text code. When they scour your site for content, the code for these images also gets noticed.

Tagging Public Images

Tagging your photos, along with appropriate titles, makes your images searchable and helps them get picked up by search engines. This can be for your own reference, or for public searches. Should you upload a photo of a mop in a kitchen, the tags on the image should be *mop* and *kitchen,* along with any other items of note that you can see in the image. Then, Flickr users who want to find a photo that corresponds to what you've posted to view or use in their own blog post can easily locate your image.

Private Images

Should you wish to upload images that are only to be shared within a select group, you can do so with Flickr. The reason for posting these images to the online service (and then marking them as private) would be perhaps to share them only with a select group of users or employees. You can determine the levels of privacy on each image, and who might have access to view them, such as those you have added as "Friends," "Family," or "Contacts" on the service. The privacy feature can be applied to an entire set or applied on a per-photo basis.

Protecting Public Content: Creative Commons Licensing

When making your content public, you do not have to give up all rights to your images, video, or even your text. Online content can be protected using a Creative Commons license (http://creativecommons.org; see Figure 8.2).

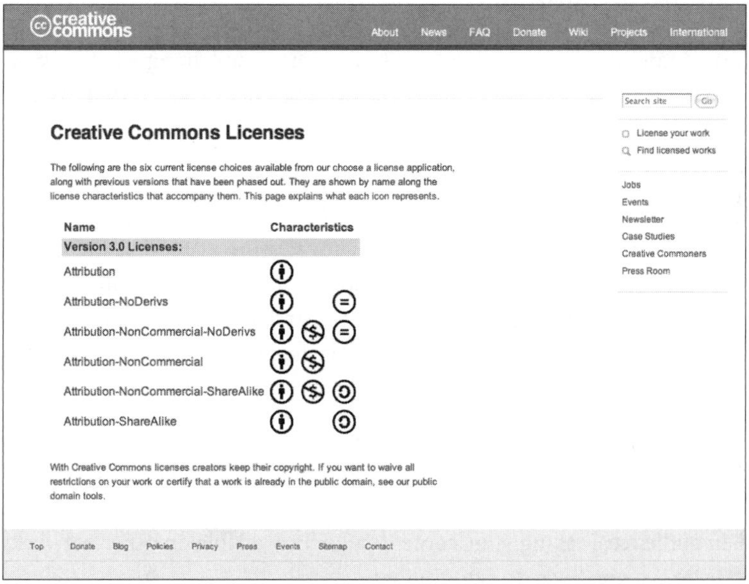

Figure 8.2 *The Creative Commons licenses.*

Creative Commons offers several levels of licenses, which have the following names:

- **Attribution**:
  This means that your images may be used (embedded) by others in their blog posts as long as they link to your blog, state your company's

name (or photographer's name), or link back to your Flickr account. You can publicly state what "attribution" levels you would like for your company on your Flickr account profile.

- **Attribution - No Derivative Works**:
  With the No Derivative Works license you are giving the public free-dom to use your images (with Attribution as outlined above) but you are also limiting them by requesting the images not be altered or used to create other works (such as a collage or another image).

- **Attribution - Noncommercial, No Derivative Works**:
  Adding the Noncommercial license to the mix means that users may use your works but not in a commercial capacity, whereas they stand to profit from using your images in advertising, for example.

- **Attribution - Noncommercial, Share Alike**:
  With Share Alike added to your license, you are giving users the per-mission to create derivative works, but only if they in turn use the same Creative Commons license on that work as you have placed on the original.

- **Attribution - Share Alike**

Creative Commons outlines each level of license by explaining whether you are allowing users to share, remix, or reuse your content and to what extent commercially.

Flickr, for example, offers several levels of Creative Commons licenses that can be preset for your entire account or modified on a per-photo basis. These licenses tell other users that your content is unavailable for sharing or republishing, or that it is free to be shared but under certain conditions. These conditions allow the reader to use or repurpose the image if it's for noncommercial use, or they may be free to share it simply by giving attribution to the original source. Creative Commons licenses exist for audio, video, images, and text content online.

YouTube is currently the king of online video. Uploading company videos, presen-tations, or interviews can help you reach out to this vast audience that has recently passed more than a billion views. If the goal of your blog is to find readers and build an audience, making your content publicly available on other networks such as YouTube is a great way to achieve that.

Using appropriate tags and titles is key with YouTube; according to recent studies, it is now the second largest search engine in the world. Using tags and keywords when providing details of your video on the network is also important to having it come up in applicable search results among all the others. Although it has a huge audience, YouTube is not the only video player or video-sharing network on the block. There are also services such as Viddler.com that enable you to watermark your logo on your videos (as shown in Figure 8.3).

Figure 8.3 *Videos from Powermat on Viddler video-sharing network.*

Vimeo.com is another video service that caters to top-quality, high-definition videos. All of these services enable you to title, tag, sort, subscribe, and embed your videos elsewhere. Clips up to 90 seconds in length can also be added to Flickr, which can also handle HD videos.

Audio

Adding audio to a blog post can bring life to an interview, event, or allow you to publish weekly podcast updates. As with writing blog posts, the length of the audio clip or podcast should be taken into consideration. Podcast episodes should be about 10 to 20 minutes in length and the same applies for an interview. Bear in mind your listeners will be spending that length of time on your site as the audio plays or if they have downloaded the audio podcast, they may be listening during their commute. Keeping their attention while not making them commit to an extremely long sound bite is key.

Attaching audio to a blog post can add a lot to the content if you can find the appropriate service to help you get set up. When putting audio in your blog post or when uploading it to a service, be sure to always add tags and keyword descriptions so that it can get picked up by search engines looking for text.

Following are two online services to which you can upload audio files or record and share audio:

- Utterli is an audio service where you can record directly from their site, or they can give you a phone number to call and it will record voice memos directly from your phone. These voice memos or direct phone calls to Utterli are then posted on your online account for you to share or save.

- PodBean.com is an online service that allows you to upload or record and share audio clips of any length (see Figure 8.4). Once your audio is recorded or if you upload an audio file you recorded on your computer, you can then copy and paste the provided embedding code into your blog post. This will then launch an audio player that will play your audio.

Figure 8.4 *PodBean.com audio and podcasting service.*

With PodBean, you can also convert your audio files or playlists into a podcast. *Podcasts* are audio files or shows to which users can subscribe. By subscribing using RSS feeds, users can be notified of new uploads or episodes through iTunes. iTunes will let you know if there are new episodes from a podcast and ask whether you want to download them. This way your readers or listeners automatically get notified when you have produced new content. Promoting your blog or including your blog's Web address on these services and in the details of each audio clip will help drive that audience to your site, where they can get more information from your company.

Other

Another unique tool for sharing content online is Slideshare (http://slideshare.net). It enables you to upload your slideshow presentations online, where they can be tagged, commented on, and put into an embeddable player (see Figure 8.5).

Figure 8.5 *Slideshare.net online slide-sharing social network.*

After you present a slideshow at a conference or meeting, audience members might want to reference your slides later or gather information they couldn't catch the first time around. If you make your slides available online, members of the audience have a reason to reach out to you after the conference has ended.

Slideshare works with PowerPoint or other slideshow application files, and you can also add audio notes or text to explain the slides on the site. Slideshows can be embedded in your blog, just like a regular video, so you can direct people to your blog as a follow-up. Slides can be viewed individually, as a show, or in full-screen mode.

Private or Members-Only Content

Including public content in a blog is ideal, but there is something to be said for rewarding your loyal fans or readers with special members-only deals or exclusive access to your content. Businesses offer loyalty or points cards with special offers, and sports fans or fans of radio or TV shows can sign up to receive exclusive content online. You can offer the same type of exclusive content to registered members, or perhaps those who have signed up for your e-mail newsletters.

Locking down your entire site or all of your images is not recommended. After all, your goal is to drive traffic to your blog. However, creating a special hidden page that is publicized to a select group only is one way to offer unique content to loyal followers. You can also make this exclusive content available for a limited time, which may help you run campaigns and track statistics. For example, if you have a special new logo or image that others might want to see, you could send the private Web link to your fan base or e-mail subscribers. Let them know the content is up for only a limited time, and then you can pull the content after a week or two and collect data for that period of time, such as number of clickthroughs from the e-mail, the number of visitors to the private site link, and so on.

Keep in mind that whatever content you supply to this special section should also be content you wouldn't mind having in the public realm. *Always* assume that anything uploaded or posted online (if even behind a password) will show up in the public space at some point.

Another example is a recording artist who is releasing a new album. He or she can preview a new song on a blog by streaming the audio. The artist could send out an e-mail or simply publish a blog post about the exclusive sneak peak that will take place for a certain amount of time. When fans receive the e-mail or notice the blog post, they can come check it out. Those who miss out on the offer will pay close attention next time, and those who were lucky enough to catch it will be that much more faithful to the site.

Podcasting

As noted earlier, podcasts are audio files that are made available by subscription. Just as a reader would subscribe to a blog, the reader can also subscribe to a podcast by RSS feed. The podcaster sets up the feed so that when they upload and publish a new episode, subscribers are alerted through services such as iTunes. Listeners can then download the episode on their computers or put it directly on their portable audio players.

Contrary to what the name of the medium suggests, you do not need an iPod specifically to listen to a podcast. Some argue the word *pod* could stand for "portable on demand," which is exactly how listeners access the audio.

As mentioned in the "Audio" section earlier in this chapter, you can use online services such as PodBean to record, upload, and manage your audio files, but you can also do this through blog posts. Embedding this audio in your blog posts still allows your main blog readers to see this content on your site and to get it automatically if they are subscribed to your main blog RSS feed.

Creating and Promoting Podcasts

When deciding to publish a podcast or a series of audio clips/episodes, it is just as important to determine the subject matter of the audio as it is when you are thinking about content for your blog posts.

If you can record audio onto your computer, you can create a podcast. Popular programs include Audacity for Windows users (http://audacity.sourceforge.net) or Übercaster (http://www.ubercaster.com) for those using a Mac (see Figure 8.6). Apple's Garage Band (http://www.apple.com/ilife/garageband/) can also be used for podcast production on Mac computers.

Figure 8.6 *Audio recording with Übercaster.*

Show Notes

Should you decide to turn your audio clips into episodes or a series, you can create show notes to help you stay on track.

Show notes are items of information in the order in which you will be talking about them on your audio file. For example, if your goal is to talk about a new product and then interview its creator, you can use the following show notes for guidance:

- Introduction

- Product overview

- Introduce guest/interviewee

- Summary

After you have recorded your audio and uploaded it to a service such as PodBean or through your blog platform, you can then embed the audio in a blog post, much like how you would embed a YouTube video. In the blog post, you can include your show notes and also put in links, such as a Web link to the product or to the interviewee.

Music

If you want to add more to your audio podcast, you can enhance your clips with music. Adding full songs or background music that plays while you speak can spruce up the audio, making it sound more robust to the audience. These pieces of audio or introduction music in your podcast can break up and enhance the speaking portion, just as images break up text on a screen.

Commercial music contains strict usage licenses, but you can look to "pod-safe" music to include in your episodes. Music with this distinction is licensed to specifically permit use in podcast production.

MusicAlley (formerly the Podsafe Music Network) is a great resource that provides a list of artists and songs that can be safely used in podcasting (http://www.musicalley.com). You can search by artist, genre, or see what others have been listening to in the Most Listens section.

Editing and Publishing

You can add music to your audio using the podcasting programs and services previously listed. With programs such as Übercaster, you can control the volume levels on each audio track. Your voice would be track one, and the music track two. For background music, simply fade down the volume level on track two so that your voice in track one stands out.

After your audio is recorded and background music is added in as you see fit, use the features in your audio recording program to add album art, titles, and tags. You can then export your audio MP3 file, or with a program such as Übercaster you can upload it directly to a server online.

From there, you can go to Podblaze (http://www.podblaze.com) to create your RSS feed. However, if you will be using your blog to publish the audio, you might only need to add the audio to a blog post and then submit your blog feed as a podcast feed. With WordPress, for example, a plug-in called PodPress enables you to upload and add your audio to blog posts. They are then displayed in custom players in your posts. You can then go to a service such as Feed2Podcast (http://feed2pod-cast.com) to identify that there will be a podcast or audio included in your regular blog feed.

The same can be done with FeedBurner (http://www.feedburner.com), by Google, to create your podcast feed (see Figure 8.7). They have a specific button for you to check that reads "I Am a Podcaster!" after you enter your blog URL or existing feed.

Figure 8.7 *Creating your podcast feed with FeedBurner.*

After everything has been verified, you should be able to publish a blog post that includes your audio file, and your feed will then display the audio button.

Be sure to promote your podcast feed on your blog so that users can subscribe to it separately, or alongside the blog feed.

To build your audience outside of your blog, you can bring in more readers through podcasting networks. You can add your podcast to a wide variety of directories, including the most popular, iTunes. Through a simple step-by-step process, you can submit your podcast feed to be listed in the global iTunes directory, as shown in Figure 8.8.

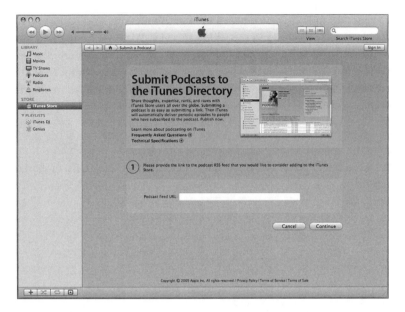

Figure 8.8 *Submitting your podcast feed to the iTunes directory.*

By submitting your podcast feed to iTunes, you not only make it easier for listeners to get your audio (and in turn come back to your blog for more information), you also open up your blog to the entire iTunes audience. Podcasts are sorted into directories on iTunes, so you can gain a new blog reader if someone comes across your podcast and wants to find out more about your company online. By putting more content out to more services, sites, and directories, you can expect to see more of an audience come back to your blog.

Screencasts

Screencasts are videos that capture what's happening on your computer's screen. These are ideal for product demos and tutorials because screencast-capturing programs enable you to use microphone audio to walk your audience through the workflow on your screen. After you have recorded your screen and saved the video file, you can then upload it to YouTube or other sharing services as a fully embeddable video.

On a Mac, you can use an application such as ScreenFlow to record video of whatever you have on your computer screen. For Windows computers, you can use Camtasia, which also enables you to highlight and zoom in on certain parts of your screen. Providing these guided tours in video format can lead to an entire blog series of "how to" video screencasts or demos that your customers may find useful.

Creating and Promoting Screencasts

To create a screencast demo, you can write up a formal script or just do a walk-through of what you would like to capture. Programs for recording on your screen include Camtasia (http://www.techsmith.com/camtasia.asp) for Windows users, and ScreenFlow, which comes with Macs that are running Leopard (or later). Snapz Prox (http://www.ambrosiasw.com/utilities/snapzprox) is also available for Mac users.

These programs enable you to record your computer screen and the actions you make, such as browsing Web sites or using other applications. They can record your computer's audio or audio from a microphone. You can also include your cursor movements in the screencast, which may prove handy for demos, or you can remove the cursor.

Applications such as OmniDazzle (http://www.omnigroup.com/applications/omnidazzle) can add graphic elements to your screencasts by attaching animations, such as a spotlight or color-coding, to your cursor onscreen.

After you have recorded your screencast, it can be treated like any other video. You can upload it through your blogging platform or publish it on video-sharing Web sites. Be sure to include appropriate titles and tags for your screencast, including the tag *screencast*.

Uploading your screencast to a video-sharing network is just as valuable as sharing other forms of multimedia or video, as there is an audience for that type of content online. Since August 2009, for example, there have been 12,500 videos tagged as *screencast* on YouTube, and 17,300 tagged as *screencasting*. If a user wants more information, a demo, or a tutorial video, he will most likely head to YouTube and find your screencast demo when it shows up in the search listings that direct users to your content.

When you are recording your screencast, be sure to begin and end the video with your company's name and how people can find out more, including a visual of your blog or blog URL. Putting content out on other networks reaches broader audiences but you still want to let them know how to come back to your official home base (that is, your blog).

Case Study: Blendtec

In 2006, Blendtec, a manufacturer of blenders that has been in operation since 1975, took to the YouTube airwaves with a video demonstrating the powerful blending capabilities of its product.

As they put a bag of 50 marbles into the Blendtec Total Blender and turned it on, the question that was asked on the video was this: Will it blend? The response to the video online was overwhelming, and since that time, they have created 90 videos, and the original marble video currently has almost four million views on YouTube.

At first, the series looked like a prank, tossing items into a blender to see how badly they could get chopped up. But the audience quickly realized that in this safe, controlled environment, Tom Dickson, the company's founder, was simply selling his product in an original way.

Dickson has since been featured in his lab coat in all 90 videos by Blendtec produced over the years. They were the first to "blend" an iPhone upon its release in 2007, and that video is their most popular, with more than seven million YouTube views to date (see Figure 8.9).

Figure 8.9 Blentec's Will it Blend? YouTube channel: http://www.youtube.com/blendtec.

Some simply enjoy watching the product being tested, whereas others like to see if it can truly blend something like Silly Putty, pens, or a crowbar.

Will it Blend? went *viral*, meaning that it was shared and passed along through social networks like Digg and that videos have been embedded on countless blogs. The official WillItBlend.com website prominently features the Total Blender and shows you how to go about making a purchase (see Figure 8.10). It also sells Will It

Blend? merchandise, making it an official Internet pop-culture hit. Tom Dickson has also been asked to make national broadcast appearances to demonstrate the Total Blender's capabilities.

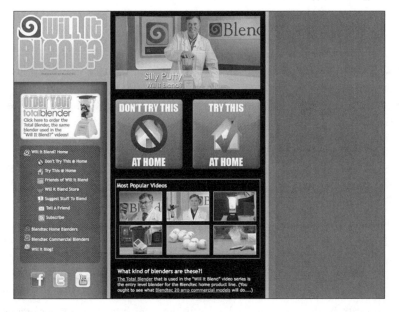

Figure 8.10 *Blentec's Will it Blend? Web site.*

The videos were uploaded to the video-sharing service Revver, which allows its users to earn revenue by posting their content. According to *USA Today* (http://www.usatoday.com/tech/webguide/internetlife/2007-09-13-revver_N.htm) in September 2007, the Will It Blend? series earned the second highest annual payout from Revver (about $15,000).

Will It Blend? doesn't stop with video. They also have a blog (Will It Blog?). This blog features the video series, and it provides general information about their products. On the blog, they open up the Total Blender and deconstruct it to show how it all works and how it has the power to blend even a set of skis. They also feature other blenders, ways to clean your product, and company or product updates.

According to Blendtec.com, in 1975 Tom Dickson "revolutionized the way homemakers would forever mill wheat into flour." The Will It Blend? video series reached out to an entire audience it may not have had prior to 2006.

Since then, Blendtec blenders have been used for baking, smoothies, and now... golf balls. Appealing to the YouTube audience introduced the product to a whole new generation of customers.

Before the video series, most of the younger generation never gave any thought to the brand of blender they would purchase or recommend. But thanks to these clever and entertaining marketing efforts, the company is thriving, most likely in part because of the combined 83 million views on its Will It Blend? videos.

Summary

By adding multimedia, you can further promote and publicize your blog's great content to audiences of millions around the globe. Your blog might not have many visitors when you first start writing, but by adding photos and video to online networks with millions, if not billions of views, you tap into a whole new audience pool.

Encouraging others to embed your multimedia helps your readers and followers spread your message, and in turn, you can promote their contributions by featuring their Creative Commons licensed photos on your blog or Flickr group.

Each reader and audience member is unique and will come to your blog for the writing, the photos, or for the videos you embed within your posts. Some like to get their information visually, and others audibly. You can cater to these different preferences by using multimedia on your blog and by sharing it on other networks. Your goal is to get those viewers, listeners, and readers to return to your blog. That's your priority. By driving them back to your blog, which is your number one online source, you will not only nurture your current audience, you'll also watch it grow.

9

Taking Advantage of Web 3.0 Blogs

As I write this, a news article has appeared on the CNN Web site stating that the one millionth word in the English language is Web 2.0, according to the Global Language Monitor Web site (http://www.languagemonitor.com), a site that documents, analyzes, and tracks trends in language. It's really no surprise that Web 2.0 is now part of the lexicon because the term is everywhere.

So what is Web 2.0? It's a set of technologies that took hold in the 2000s and includes collaboration-based services such as blogging and social networking to help people connect on the Web, not just obtain information from static Web sites. Web 1.0 denoted Web sites with content that was driven from the top down. In contrast, Web 2.0 describes the decentralization of Web content, where information is provided from bottom-up sources such as bloggers and the people who comment on blog posts.

Seeds of the next generation of Web technology were planted before that technology blossomed. Blogging started in the late 1990s and became popular in the 2000s. And as we begin the second decade of the twenty-first century, we're seeing the seeds of Web 3.0 technologies being planted.

For example, Reed Hastings, the founder and CEO of Netflix, described Web 3.0 as being the full-video Web that will be made possible by the increasing growth in bandwidth available to customers that will allow transmission of full movies over the Web (http://en.wikipedia. org/wiki/Web_1.0).

Eric Schmidt, the CEO of Google, also gave a good definition of Web 3.0 at a conference in Seoul, South Korea, in 2007. He stated that Web 3.0 will be small, fast applications "in the cloud" (that is, available on the Internet) that can run on any device (PC or mobile) and are distributed through social networks and other Web 2.0 technologies (http://www.readwriteweb.com/archives/eric_schmidt_defines_web_30.php).

It's hard to get a handle on Web 3.0 technologies when businesses are already trying to digest what Web 2.0 technologies have to offer. Businesses trying to stay ahead of the curve (and their competition) by investigating Web 3.0 technologies are hampered further because people can't agree on a definition for Web 3.0. This lack of a definition causes businesses to check out a wide variety of potential technologies that might or might not be adopted in the future.

In this chapter, I sort through the Web 3.0 clutter, tell you what evolutionary trends are emerging, and show you how you to take advantage of "mashing up" different Web technologies.

An Overview of Web 3.0 Technologies

If you type "Web 3.0" into the Search box in your favorite search engine, you'll find several definitions:

- The Web is becoming much more mobile as PDAs and cell phone functionality merge and include access to the Internet, social networking, and anything else the user wants to do at home, according to a May 2009 research report from Forrester Research (http://www.mobile marketer.com/cms/news/research/3275.html). Apple's iPhone and Palm's Pre are just two of the latest mobile handsets that offer fast Internet connectivity no matter where you are.

- Tim Berners-Lee, director of the World Wide Web Consortium (and inventor of the Internet) described the Semantic Web (Web 3.0) as becoming "capable of analyzing all data on the Web—the content, links, and transactions between people and computers" (http://en.wikipedia.org/wiki/Semantic_Web). Berners-Lee believes that the Semantic Web will take advantage of "intelligent agents" that are autonomous entities and direct its activity toward achieving goals (http://en.wikipedia.org/wiki/Intelligent_agent). In the case of the Semantic Web, intelligent agents will crawl through the Web in response to complex questions. For example, if I want to go to a performance of the San Francisco Opera and then go to a Moroccan restaurant in the city for dinner afterward, I can ask a complex question such as "What is the next performance of the San Francisco Opera and where can I find a good Moroccan restaurant to eat afterward?" The Web will take that information and organize richer results for me than what is available today.

- The Web will become more personalized to your needs. You're probably used to shopping sites such as Amazon.com learning about your past purchases and offering suggestions based on those purchases the next time you shop on their site. In a Web 3.0 world, your browser will learn over time what your preferences are and will tailor your browsing experiences to your preferences. What's more, everyone's browsing experience will be different even when they go to the same URL. The Amazon.com Web site already does this to some degree. When you visit Amazon.com, the site uses browser cookies to determine what you looked at last time you visited so that it can promote related products that you may like.

So with all this in mind, what technologies are being used right now that are forerunners of Web 3.0 technologies to come? We'll take a look at two: Wikipedia and widgets.

Wikipedia

You've probably heard of wiki Web sites. The term *wiki* means "fast" in Hawaiian, but in the Web world it means a Web site that has a number of interlinking pages that are managed using a relational database system. The pages are Spartan in looks but quick to load, and people can add and edit entries within the wiki system.

There are plenty of wiki sites available on the Web, and you can download and establish your own wiki on your own Web site. An example of the former is the popular Wikipedia site (http://www.wikipedia.org), which is a free online encyclopedia maintained by users. You can get a lot of information on Wikipedia that you might not be able to get anyplace else, such as a comparison of wiki software, as shown in Figure 9.1.

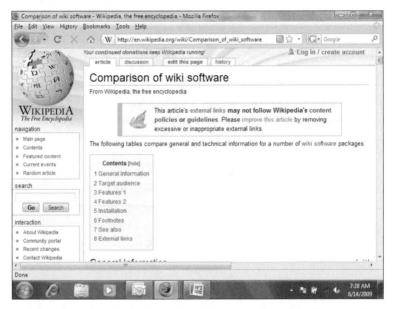

Figure 9.1   *The Wikipedia Web site page that compares wiki software packages.*

Wikis have been around since the mid-1990s, but only recently have companies started to leverage wiki technologies, along with developing Web 3.0 technologies to make data exchange more accessible to businesses. For example, the Swirrl Web site (http://www.swirrl.com) shown in Figure 9.2 is staking an early claim on being a Web 3.0 company.

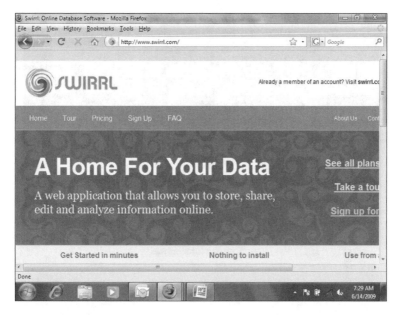

Figure 9.2 *The Swirrl Web site.*

Swirrl leverages the Semantic Web technology called Linked Data, which is the recommended best practice for exposing and linking data on the Web. (If you want to
see an example of how it works and to get more information, go to the Linked Data
Web site at http://linkeddata.org/.) Using Linked Data, Swirrl maintains your data
online so that people can log in using a modern Web browser, add information akin
to a wiki, and microblog to other people in the business or project team. Swirrl has
positioned itself to businesses as a service using tools that are familiar, easy to use,
and easy to access.

APIs and Widgets

Some Web 2.0 platforms currently in use may be the springboard for Web 3.0 technologies. For example, many social networking sites, including LinkedIn and
Facebook, offer application programming interfaces (APIs) to developers so that
they can create applications using those sites' unique resources. For example,
LinkedIn has an application that links to a person's WordPress blog.

Modern operating systems such as Mac OS X and Windows 7, as well as mobile
computing platforms like the iPhone, have established small applications called
widgets. Widgets can also be small applications that link to an object, such as a few
lines of HTML code from YouTube that you place in a blog post to show a video
presentation you gave recently. A good place to find a comprehensive list of widgets
for the desktop, the Web, and your mobile device is the Widgipedia Web site
(http://www.widgipedia.com) shown in Figure 9.3.

Figure 9.3   *The Widgipedia Web site.*

So what does this mean for your business if you're trying to reach your customers? First, you might be able to find an application available that you can use to enhance your blog, link to your Web site, and link to your social networking sites at little or no charge. What's more, developers are working to "mash up" applications to make them more usable and relevant.

Mash It Up!

The term *mash up* (also sometimes styled as mashup, but we call it mash up throughout this book for consistency) means to combine one or more applications into a single application. You might have seen an example of this on a business site (or perhaps your own business site) that lets visitors check Google Maps to see where a company is located. That's a basic example. If you want to see more interesting mash ups, look at the Webmashup.com site shown in Figure 9.4.

On this site, you can view more than 200 examples of how people combine applications into a new one. For example, one site combines the news resources of Digg, Slashdot, and del.icio.us to form doggdot.us, as shown in Figure 9.5.

Figure 9.4   *The Webmashup.com Web site.*

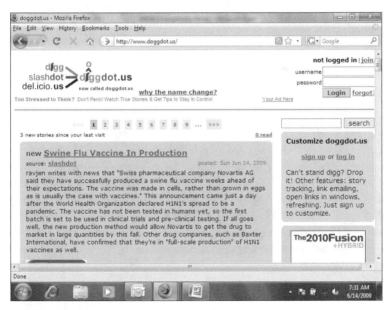

Figure 9.5   *The Doggdot.us Web site.*

This site originally included parts of the three sites it combined, but it had to change its name because of copyright issues Digg's lawyers brought to the Doggdot.us owner's attention. The cautionary note here if you have developers and you want to create your own mash up applications (such as a blog with another application) is to make sure it doesn't interfere, or give the appearance of interfering, with another company's trademarks.

There is speculation that in the future you may be able to drag and drop different programs into a Web page and have the combined application work flawlessly. For example, you could drop Google Maps and several local business and newspaper Web sites so that you can see where companies are currently building. No one has figured out how to do this as of this writing, but developers are thinking about it.

Integrating Semantic Technologies

The Semantic Web requires that ontologies, or files that define the relationships between groups of terms, be detailed and comprehensive so that the Web can find richer search results for you. The translation of "detailed and comprehensive" is a lot of work, and there's debate about whether people will be interested in putting in the work to make their Web sites as searchable as possible.

On the other hand, blogs, photoblogs, and vlogs all allow you to add tags so that you can categorize your blogs. For example, in the Halfway There blog, shown in Figure 9.6, the Blogger Web site allows you to add category tags at the bottom of the post. In this example, if you click the Journalism category tag, you'll see all posts that also have that tag.

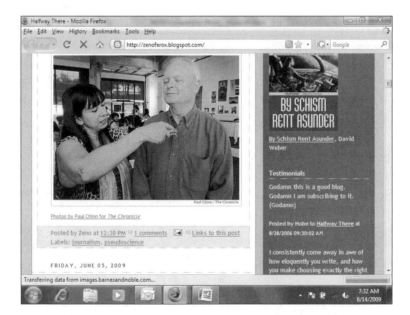

Figure 9.6 *The Halfway There blog with the Journalism category tag.*

If you're interested in integrating semantic technologies into your blog right away, blog software and sites have these tagging features so that you can add posts to one or more categories, add a category list to your blog, and make reading a little easier for people who are interested in specific topics.

Make Agents Work for Your Blog

So how do you make your Web site available to the Semantic Web and get your business ahead of the Web 3.0 curve? A company in Ireland has developed a search engine that will help get your blog and your Web site noticed, as long as you have a developer on board (or would like to program it yourself).

The Digital Enterprise Research Institute (DERI) of Galway, Ireland, has created the Sindice Semantic Web search engine at http://www.sindice.com (see Figure 9.7).

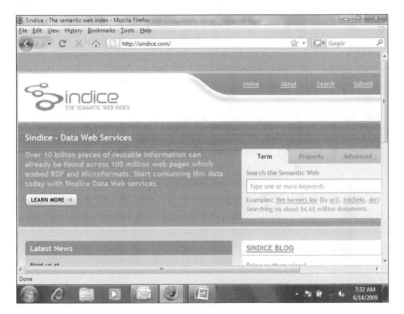

Figure 9.7   *The Sindice Web site.*

This site not only lets you search Web sites that have the Semantic Web language framework called Resource Description Framework, or RDF, but that also use Sindice APIs and widgets to integrate into your blog and other applications.

The good news is that when your Webmaster submits your blog (and even your Web site) to Sindice, the site will be indexed within an hour. So, people searching for your site will be able to find it even more quickly.

The bad news is that as of this writing Sindice is still in early beta form, and if people want to check you out on the Semantic Web, they need to visit the Sindice Web site. Even so, if you want your blog and any other Web assets to be on the cutting edge, consider making the Sindice agents work for you.

Case Study: UrbanSpoon.com

If you're looking for a place to eat in a metropolitan area near you, the UrbanSpoon.com Web site is a good place to get comprehensive information about restaurants in the area. UrbanSpoon.com, shown in Figure 9.8, is also a good example of using mash ups to create an early-generation Web 3.0 site.

Figure 9.8 *The UrbanSpoon.com Web site Sacramento listings.*

The site in this example is for the Sacramento area; however, you can choose another city at the top of the page or search for a particular term. The site has a number of different category lists from the top 10 rated restaurants overall, popular restaurants with readers who rate the restaurants, types of food, neighborhoods, features, price, and more.

Part of that "more" includes a widget that lets you select a restaurant at random in the Sacramento area if you don't know where to go, and you can put this widget on your own blog or Web site. The home page also mashes up information from local newspaper critics and local bloggers.

If you click a restaurant to check it out, you'll see a number of Web 2.0 and 3.0 features. In Figure 9.9, the Chicago Fire Pizza page on UrbanSpoon lets you interact with the listing in a number of ways.

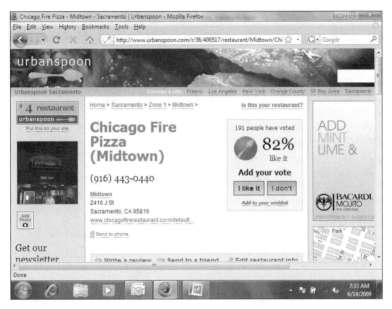

Figure 9.9   *The Chicago Fire Pizza listing on UrbanSpoon.com.*

You can write a review, view the menu, and read critic, blogger, and other user reviews. If you want to know where the restaurant is, the Google map will tell you where it is. You can also get driving directions, see nearby restaurants, and even see other pizza places if you decide Chicago Fire is not to your liking.

If you scroll down to the bottom of the page, you'll see a link to another Web 3.0 feature: the UrbanSpoon application for the iPhone. Of course, UrbanSpoon doesn't just use the iPhone; you can also get UrbanSpoon on your mobile phone. After you enter your phone number and choose your carrier, you send the number to your phone and then receive a text link.

The bottom of the page also has a link to the UrbanSpoon blog, where you can get more information about what's going on with UrbanSpoon and view food blogs by metro region.

Although there is a lot of information on UrbanSpoon.com, the ready availability of that information no matter where you are makes UrbanSpoon a good example of leveraging Web 2.0 and 3.0 technologies to give customers what they need.

Summary

The second decade of the 21st century is coming fast, and Web 3.0 technologies are coming with it. There are several different technologies that comprise the Web 3.0 definition including mobile devices, the Semantic Web that will use intelligent agents to achieve goals, and a Web much more personalized to your needs.

This chapter looked at different technologies and techniques being used that are signs of Web 3.0 technologies to come, including APIs, widgets, mashups, and adding tags to your blog. The UrbanSpoon Web site is a good example of how to use them.

Hopefully you now have enough ideas in your head to create or improve your blog so it will drive business to your company. If you want to chat with us and ask us questions, feel free to visit our Web site at www.blogging2drivebiz.com.

A

Important Blogging Sites

In addition to the blogs already discussed in this book, the following sites are important for you to visit. The sites cover various aspects of blogging, from locating blogs online that you might find of interest, to software as a service (SAAS) that provides microblogging services for your business or business groups. You can also visit the Quick Online Tips Giant Blogging Terms Dictionary for more sites and suggestions, at http://www.quickonlinetips.com/archives/2006/06/the-giant-blogging-terms-glossary/.

Technorati

If you want to know what's going on in the blogosphere, start at Technorati, at
http://www.technorati.com (see Figure A.1).

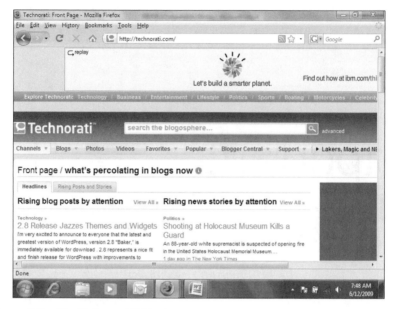

Figure A.1   *The Technorati Web site.*

News Aggregators

Bloglines (http://www.bloglines.com), shown in Figure A.2, and Newsgator
(http://www.newsgator.com), shown in Figure A.3, are two of the most popular
news aggregators. At these sites, you can read new blog posts online or download
them to your desktop.

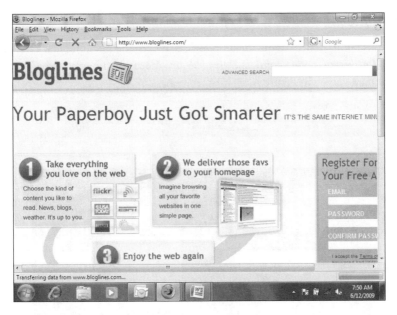

Figure A.2   *The Bloglines Web site.*

Figure A.3   *The Newsgator Web site.*

Podcatchers

If you use podcatchers to download podcasts, two of the more popular ones are
Odeo (http://www.odeo.com), shown in Figure A.4, and Podnova (http://www.pod-
nova.com), shown in Figure A.5.

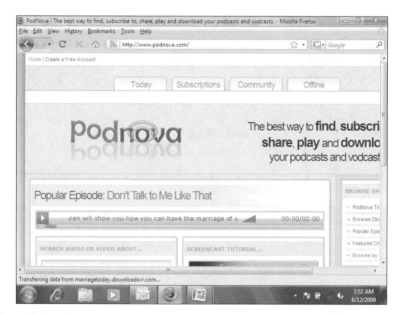

Figure A.4   *The Odeo Web site.*

Figure A.5   *The Podnova Web site.*

Ping Search Engines

If you update your blog regularly, search engines may not pick up on the update right away. You can ping search engines using online services such as Pingomatic (http://www.pingomatic.com), which is shown in Figure A.6.

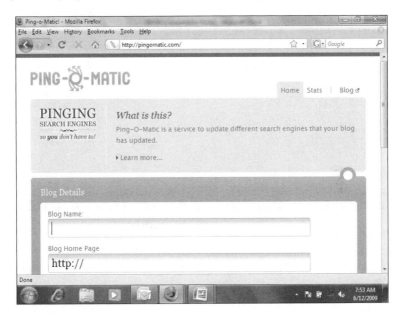

Figure A.6   *The Pingomatic Web site.*

Want to Advertise on Blogs?

If you're looking to advertise your product or service on specific blogs, check out the Blogads site (http://www.blogads.com), shown in Figure A.7, to help you develop your online blog campaign.

You can also make your blog a moneymaking venture by placing ads on the blog. The most popular advertising mechanism for doing that is Google's AdSense, shown in Figure A.8. This site, at https://www.google.com/adsense, connects your blog to Google's large group of advertisers.

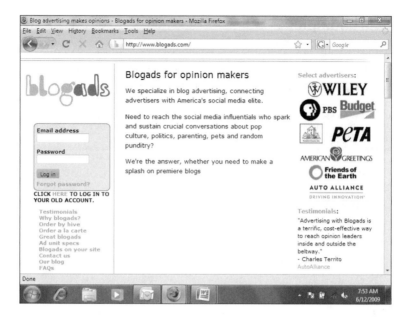

Figure A.7   *The Blogads Web site.*

Figure A.8   *The Google AdSense Web site.*

Getting More Blog Traffic

If you're interested in pushing more people to your blog, there are Web services that promise to do exactly that. Check out BlogExplosion (http://www.blogexplosion.com), shown in Figure A.9, and BlogClicker (http://www.blogclicker.com), shown in Figure A.10. Both sites let you add your blog to a community of blogs where you read other blogs and other bloggers read your blog.

You should also check out sites that let you post links to your blog. The most popular sites are Digg.com, shown in Figure A.11, and Slashdot.org, shown in Figure A.12. Digg.com allows you to send your blog post to them immediately so that users can check it out in the Upcoming Stories section and determine whether others should view it; the more Diggs your blog post has, the more likely it will be more visible on Digg.com. With Slashdot, you must submit your blog post URL so that the Slashdot editors can review it and determine whether it's worth posting on their site.

Figure A.9   *The BlogExplosion Web site.*

Figure A.10   *The BlogClicker Web site.*

Figure A.11   *The Digg Web site.*

Figure A.12   *The Slashdot Web site.*

Software as a Service Product

In its June 1, 2009 issue, *eWeek* magazine (http://www.eweek.com) published a comparison of three software as a service (SAAS) products that leverage Web 2.0 technologies, including microblogging and wikis for use in businesses. That is, these SAAS products are access-controlled for businesses, and they also compete with established programs such as Lotus Notes and Microsoft SharePoint. The three products are Socialcast, Socialtext, and Huddle.

Figure A.13 shows Socialcast (http://www.socialcast.com). This site is a Twitter-like service.

Socialtext (http://www.socialtext.com), shown in Figure A.14, started out as a site that enabled users to create wikis (for example, people in product groups can create wikis about their products) but now includes microblogging and user profiles, much like what Facebook offers.

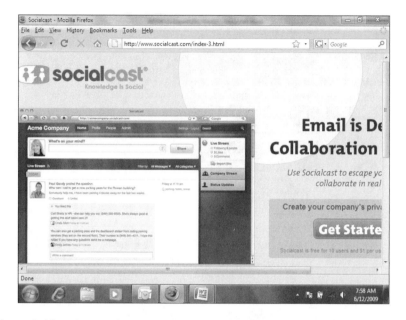

Figure A.13   *The Socialcast Web site.*

Figure A.14   *The Socialtext Web site.*

Huddle (http://www.huddle.net), shown in Figure A.15, has the most basic social networking features of the three SAAS programs, but you can use Huddle from other social networking systems and plug into other social networking sites, including Facebook and LinkedIn.

Figure A.15   *The Huddle Web site.*

Index

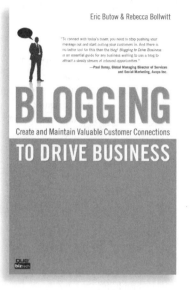

Eric Butow & Rebecca Bollwitt

"To connect with today's buyer, you need to stop pushing your message out and start pulling your customers in. And there is no better tool for this than the blog! *Blogging to Drive Business* is an essential guide for any business wishing to use a blog to attract a steady stream of inbound opportunities."
—Paul Gillin, Global Managing Director of Services and Social Marketing, Avaya Inc.

BLOGGING
Create and Maintain Valuable Customer Connections
TO DRIVE BUSINESS

FREE Online Edition

Your purchase of **Blogging to Drive Business** includes access to a free online edition for 45 days through the Safari Books Online subscription service. Nearly every Que book is available online through Safari Books Online, along with more than 5,000 other technical books and videos from publishers such as Addison-Wesley Professional, Cisco Press, Exam Cram, IBM Press, O'Reilly, Prentice Hall, and Sams.

SAFARI BOOKS ONLINE allows you to search for a specific answer, cut and paste code, download chapters, and stay current with emerging technologies.

Activate your FREE Online Edition at www.informit.com/safarifree

> **STEP 1:** Enter the coupon code: DOTJZAA.

> **STEP 2:** New Safari users, complete the brief registration form. Safari subscribers, just log in.

If you have difficulty registering on Safari or accessing the online edition, please e-mail customer-service@safaribooksonline.com

Safari
Books Online